Practical Chinese Reader
Elementary Course: Book II

Traditional Character Edition

Cheng & Tsui Company

Practical Chinese Reader
Elementary Course: Book II

Traditional Character Edition

Beijing Language Institute

Cheng & Tsui Company

Cheng & Tsui Company
25 West Street
Boston, MA 02111-1268 USA
e-mail ct@world.std.com

Traditional Character Edition 0-88727-231-2

Supplementary exercise book, writing workbook, computer software, video tapes and audio tapes
are available from the publisher.

Printed in the United States of America

Publisher's Note to 1995 Edition

With the help of our many wonderful customers, we are happy to be able to supply you with a much more thoroughly proofread and edited version of the Traditional Character Edition of *Practical Chinese Reader Book 1* and *Book 2*. In addition to correcting typographical and *pinyin* tone mark errors, we have included at the bottom of each page, in parentheses, the corresponding pages in the Simplified Character Edition. With this ready cross-reference, we hope that it will be easier to use the audio cassette tapes which refer only to page numbers in the Simplified Character Edition.

In addition, a single asterisk (*) has been placed next to characters that appear in the supplementary vocabulary list. A double asterisk (**) has been placed next to characters than can be used interchangeably with other characters. The first reference to this character gives the alternate character; see pages 1, 13, 52, 62 and 65.

We would also like to inform our readers that vocabulary indexes to these two texts are provided at the end of the respective supplement, *Practical Chinese Reader I: Patterns and Exercises* and *Practical Chinese Reader II: Patterns and Exercises.*

While we have made a concerted effort to make this edition as accurate as possible, we welcome user input and recommendations as part of our commitment to improving our products.

Publisher's Note to the First Edition

The Cheng & Tsui Company is pleased to make available the first two volumes of the traditional (or full) character edition of the *Practical Chinese Reader,* the highly successful introductory Chinese language textbook compiled by the Beijing Language Institute and published by the Commercial Press.

The Beijing Language Institute, the leading institution teaching Chinese as a foreign language in the People's Republic of China, produces many significant and valuable language texts. Unfortunately, many of these texts have not been widely known or available in the West. The *C&T Asian Language Series* is designed to publish and widely distribute quality language texts as they are completed by teachers at leading educational institutions, such as the Beijing Language Institute.

While the substantive text in this Traditional Character Edition is unchanged, we have made some editorial judgments, so that the book does not correspond page for page to the original Simplified Character Edition. Specifically, we give all explanatory material in English only; nonessential pictures are not always included or in the same place as in the simplified edition; and we have deleted the "Table of Stroke Order of Chinese Characters" in each lesson and compiled them in a separate volume entitled *Practical Chinese Reader I and II: Writing Workbook,* in which students can practice writing.

Additionally, we have also published the supplements *Practical Chinese Reader I: Patterns and Exercises* and *Practical Chinese Reader II: Patterns and Exercises* to provide the grammatical reinforcement lacking in the primary texts.

We would like to note that were it not for the tireless efforts of Professor Shou-hsin Teng, the Chief Editor of our Editorial Board, this Traditional Character Edition of *Practical Chinese Reader* might never have been published, and certainly not in its present complete and attractively typeset form.

Finally, we sincerely invite readers' comments and suggestions concerning the publications in this series. If you have comments or suggestions, please contact the following members of the Editorial Board:

Professor Shou-hsin Teng, Chief Editor
Dept. of Asian Languages and Literature
University of Massachusetts, Amherst, MA 01003

Professor Samuel Cheung
Dept. of East Asian Languages, University of California, Berkeley, CA 94720

Professor Ying-che Li
Dept. of East Asian Languages, University of Hawaii, Honolulu, HI 96822

Professor Timothy Light
Dept. of Religion, Western Michigan University, Kalamazoo, MI 49008

Professor Ronald Walton
Dept. of Hebrew and East Asian Languages and Literature
University of Maryland, College Park, MD 20742

Introduction

Practical Chinese Reader is designed for foreign learners of elementary Chinese, primarily in a classroom setting, although it may also be used as a self-study course of modern Mandarin Chinese.

The fifty lessons in Books I and II aim to teach the communication of everyday Chinese and to lay a solid foundation for further Chinese language studies. These goals are accomplished by means of pattern substitution, functional item drills, grammatical analysis and various types of multiple-purpose exercises.

This course is devised on the following principles:

1. The texts are prepared in current, standard, and idiomatic modern Chinese, as spoken by native speakers. Priority is given to the most essential language items that the learner will need to express himself in everyday Chinese conversation.

2. This course aims not only to teach the learner speech forms, but more importantly enables the learner to use speech forms freely in specific situations. The situations involve two foreign students, Palanka and Gubo, who studied Chinese first in their country and then in China, where they make friends with native speakers. In Book I, Palanka and Gubo are represented as living in another part of the world, with the goal of enabling the learner to use Chinese in his own country.

3. Since it is important for adult learners to observe the basic rules of pronunciation and grammar, the textbook emphasizes language practice. Care has also been taken to include information respecting Chinese phonetics and grammar.

4. In order to ensure good results in language study, it is necessary for the learner to have some understanding of China's culture and history and present-day condition. For this purpose, background information on Chinese society, history, scenic spots, historical sites, local customs and conditions has been incorporated wherever possible. This information has been primarily incorporated into Book II.

5. The vocabulary, sentence patterns and their extensions, grammar, texts, reading texts and exercises in each lesson are arranged to ensure the recurrence of basic vocabulary and sentence patterns.

Since student backgrounds vary greatly, the teacher is given considerable flexibility to adapt the book to the needs of actual learners. He may use the book in whole or

i

only in part, or change the order of the presentation.

Guide to the Book:

Text: Most of the texts are written in dialogue format, which facilitates audio-lingual practice and provides an overall grounding in reading and writing elementary Chinese.

New Words: Apart from the required lexical items, an optional list of words and expressions is included in each lesson.

Notes: Following each text are a number of notes that explain difficult sentences and expressions, give additional explanations about grammar items already covered, and provide necessary background information. Although some difficult sentences may contain grammar items that are dealt with in later lessons, the students are merely required to understand these sentences.

Pronunciation Drills (included in Lessons 1-12) **and Pronunciation and Intonation:** Apart from their focal task of providing practice in conversation and basic sentence patterns, the first twelve lessons contain a concentrated dose of drills in pronunciation and tones, with an emphsasis on items that have proven difficult for foreign learners. This type of drill, which is meant to give the learner a reasonably good grounding in phonetics, continues through each lesson. Intonation drills are also added.

Conversation Practice (included in Lessons 1-12) **and Substitution and Extension:** The mechanical substitutional drills aim to give the learner a proficient but formal mastery of basic sentence patterns. These are followed by situational extension type drills, which are designed to enable the learner to use the sentence patterns with reasonable freedom.

Phonetics (included in Lessons 1-12) **and Grammar:** The phonetics and grammar items included in this book are not treated in a comprehensive and systematic manner, but are dealt with in a way that best solves the specific difficulties of the foreign learners. Due attention has also been given to peculiarities of the Chinese language. The short grammatical summary included in the revision lesson following each unit recapitulates the items that have been taught up to that point.

Reading Text: These texts are designed to ensure the recurrence of some of the vocabulary items and sentence patterns already taught, as well as to develop the students' reading comprehension and consecutive speaking and writing skills.

Exercises: The various types of exercises are designed to consolidate the main grammar items covered, including the vocabulary items dealt with in the notes. It is hoped that students will make full use of the illustrations for situational oral practice.

Characters: The "Table of Stroke-Order of Chinese Characters" in each lesson of the Simplified Character Edition has been deleted from this Traditional Charcter Edition. This information is compiled in a separate workbook entitled *Practical Chinese Reader I and II: Writing Workbook,* which allows students to practice writing.

We gratefully acknowledge the teachers of the Beijing Language Institute, who offered generous advice and assistance in the preparation of *Practical Chinese Reader* Book I and II. Teachers and students both at home and abroad are earnestly invited to offer criticisms and suggestions. This critique will be invaluable to the revision of these two volumes and the preparation of future volumes.

These books are translated into English by He Peihui, Xiong Wenhua and Mei Xiuxian, and illustrated by Jin Tingting and Zhang Zhizhong.

–Compilers
February 1981

PRACTICAL CHINESE READER
Book Two
Traditional Character Edition

TABLE OF CONTENTS

Page

第三十一課

一、課 文

我們學了兩年的中文了

（在飛機上）

古　波：請問，您是中國人嗎？

老華僑：是啊，我是華僑，從美國來。你們中國話說得不錯，學了幾年的中文了？

古　波：哪裏**，還差得遠呢。我們學了兩年中文了。

帕蘭卡：您在美國很長時間了吧？

老華僑：我在美國已經四十多年了。

古　波：您常回中國嗎？

老華僑：不，這是第二次。一九六五年我第一次回國，參觀了工廠、農村和很多學校，在上海住了三個多月。

帕蘭卡：您在美國作什麼工作？

老華僑：在大學工作。我教書已經教了三十多年了。

古　波：您家裏**還有人在北京嗎？

老華僑：有。我弟弟、妹妹都在北京。他們正在為實現四個現

** 裏 is interchangeable with 裡

— 1 —

(1,2,3)

代化努力工作。我這次回國看看，希望能為社會主義建設作一點事兒。

帕蘭卡：古波，還有五分鐘就要到北京了。

古　波：再見吧，老先生。

老華僑：再見，祝你們學習好，身體好。

帕蘭卡：謝謝！

（在首都國際機場）

張華光：請問，你是古波同學嗎？

古　波：對，我叫古波，她叫帕蘭卡。我們要去北京語言學院學習。

張華光：太好了！我是北京語言學院的學生代表，我叫張華光。這位是趙同志。

趙同志：歡迎你們！路上辛苦了，你們坐了多長時間的飛機？

帕蘭卡：坐了十幾個小時。北京的天氣真好。

趙同志：是啊，今天天氣不錯。手續辦了嗎？

古　波：手續都辦了。

趙同志：好，請大家上車吧。

二、生　詞

1. 老　　　　lǎo　　　　old; aged

2. 華僑　　　huáqiáo　　overseas Chinese

3. 話	huà	word; talk
4. 長	cháng	long
5. 時間	shíjiān	(the duration of) time; (a point of) time
6. 已經	yǐjing	already
7. 第	dì	a prefix indicating order
8. 次	cì	a measure word, time
9. 學校	xuéxiào	school
10. 大學	dàxué	university; college
11. 實現	shíxiàn	to realize; to achieve
12. 現代化	xiàndàihuà	modernization
13. 希望	xīwàng	to hope; to wish; hope; wish
14. 社會主義	shèhuìzhǔyì	socialism
15. 建設	jiànshè	to build; to construct; construction
16. 鐘	zhōng	clock
17. 首都	shǒudū	capital of a country
18. 國際	guójì	international
19. 語言	yǔyán	language
20. 同志	tóngzhì	comrade
21. 路	lù	road; way
22. 辛苦	xīnkǔ	hard; exhausting; with much toil

23.小時	xiǎoshí	hour
24.天氣	tiānqì	weather
25.手續	shǒuxù	formalities, paper work

專　名

1.美國	Měiguó	the United States (of America)
2.上海	Shànghǎi	Shanghai
3.首都國際機場	Shǒudū Guójì Jīchǎng	the Capital International Airport, Beijing
4.北京語言學院	Běijīng Yǔyán Xuéyuàn	Beijing Language Institute
5.張華光	Zhāng Huáguāng	name of a person
6.趙	Zhào	a surname

補　充　詞 **

1.錄音	lù yīn	to record (sound, voice); recording
2.一會兒	yíhuìr	a little while; in a moment
3.開會	kāi huì	to hold or to attend a meeting
4.護照	hùzhào	passport
5.拉	lā	to play (string instruments)
6.小提琴	xiǎotíqín	violin

** An asterisk (*) is used to denote items from the supplementary vocabulary list.

7. 不用   bú yòng   there is no need to

三、閱讀短文

不 認 識 的 朋 友

在火車上，一個男孩子正在認真地拉小提琴*。他拉得非常好，大家都想知道他是誰的孩子。這時候，一位老同志問他："孩子，你叫什麼名字？去哪兒？"

他回答說："我叫趙華，去北京考(kǎo to sit for an examination) 音樂學校。"

"你學了多長時間的小提琴*了？"

"我學了六年了。"

"你家在哪兒？"

"我家在雲南 (Yúnnán Yunnan Province)"

"你跟誰一起去北京？"

"我一個人去。"

老同志看了看這個孩子，又問他："你在北京有認識的人嗎？"

"沒有。"

"從雲南到北京路很遠，你爸爸媽媽應該送你去。"

"我爸爸是工人，媽媽是服務員。他們現在工作都很忙，沒有時間送我。我今年已經十一歲了，不用*他們送。"

「好，很好！」老同志笑了。他想了想，又說：「我有個姐姐在北京，你到北京以後去找她吧。吃飯、住房子的事兒，她會幫助你。這是她的地址。」

「謝謝您！」

「不用謝。我要下 (xià to get off) 車了，我去給她打個電話。」停了停，他又說：「孩子，有志者事竟成，祝你一路平安，再見！」

「謝謝您，再見。」

那位老同志是誰？他是音樂學院的老師，一位有名的音樂家。

四、注釋　Notes

1. "你們中國話說得不錯。"

"中國話" stands for "漢語". In colloquial speech it refers to spoken Chinese.

2. "哪裡，還差得遠呢。"

"Oh, far from it!" or "It's very kind of you to say so, but I really don't deserve it."

"還差得遠呢" is also a modest reply to a praise.

3. "不，這是第二次。"

"第", a prefix, can be used before a cardinal numeral to form an ordinal numeral. A measure word, however, should be inserted between the cardinal numeral and the following noun, e.g. "第一本書", "第四個星期", "第二次" and "第三十一課". Sometimes a cardinal numeral may also be used to indicate order as found in "四樓" or "四二三號", etc.

4. "他們正在為實現四個現代化努力工作。"

Here "四個現代化" is a simplified way of saying the modernizations of agriculture, industry, national defence, science and technology.

5. "還有五分鐘就要到北京了。"

"There are only five minutes to go before we arrive in Beijing."

"三分鐘", "一刻鐘" and "兩小時" are used to indicate a period of time, while "兩點四十分", "三點一刻" or "四點" refers to a point of time.

6. "路上辛苦了。"

"A tiring journey you've had, I suppose?"

"路上" means "on the way". "路上辛苦了" is used to greet a person who has just arrived from afar.

7. "你們坐了多長時間的飛機？"

"How long did it take you to fly here?"

The adverb "多" often goes before monosyllabic adjectives such as

　　　　　　　(7,8,9)

"大", "長", "遠" and "快" to ask about degree or extent, e.g. "你今年多大" "這條路多長？"

五、替換與擴展 Substitution and Extension

(一)

1. 下午你工作了嗎?
   我工作了。
   你工作了幾個小時?
   我工作了三個小時。

鍛鍊，	一個
玩兒，	半個
復習，	一個半
睡，	兩個
參觀，	三個

2. 他在上海住了幾個月?
   他在上海住了三個月。

首都，	兩個月
農村，	半個月
學校，	一年
工廠，	半年

3. 那位同志教書教了多長時間?
   他教書教了三十多年。

訪問，	中國，	兩個多星期
坐，	車，	七個多小時
辦，	手續，	十五分鐘
釣，	魚，	三個多小時
聽，	錄音*，	半天

4. 你學了幾年（的）中文了？
   我學了兩年（的）中文了。
   你學得真不錯。
   哪裡，還差得遠呢。

教，	語言課，	十五年
當，	翻譯，	兩年多
開，	車，	二十多年
研究，	中國文學，	四年

5. 他們跳舞跳了一個晚上嗎？
   他們沒有跳一個晚上，
   他們跳了半個多小時。

看電視，	一個下午，	十幾分鐘
聽音樂，	一個上午，	一刻鐘
踢足球，	一個多小時，	一會兒*
開會*，	兩個小時，	一個多小時
談話，	很長時間，	幾分鐘

6. 這本詞典你要用很長時間嗎？
   我不要用很長時間，
   我要用三天。

那些雜誌，	看，	兩天
今天的練習，	作，	三刻鐘
那些東西，	整理，	一個晚上
這本書，	翻譯，	兩個多月

(10,11,12)

1. Going through one's customs formalities

    A：請讓我看看您的護照＊。

    B：好。這是我的護照＊。

    A：您有幾件行李？

    B：兩件。裏邊都是自己用的東西。

    A：有煙、酒嗎？

    B：有幾包 (bāo packet) 煙，沒有酒。

    A：有要報關 (bàoguān to declare) 的東西嗎？

    B：沒有。

2. Meeting somebody at the airport

    A：請問，您是從中國來的趙先生嗎？

    B：是的，我叫趙辛。您是——

    A：我叫加里·謝里夫，是外語學院的代表。歡迎您到
    我們學院工作。

    B：謝謝。認識您，我很高興。

    A：路上好嗎？

    B：很好。在地圖上北京離這兒很遠，可是我們坐了十
    多個小時的飛機就到了。

    A：希望您在這兒過得很好。

    B：謝謝您。

3. Talking about a plan

    A：你準備在中國學習幾年？

B：我準備在中國學習三年。我希望能到北京大學中文系學習現代文學。

A：第一年你就去北（京）大（學）嗎？

B：不。我想在語言學院學習半年漢語。我的口語不太好，我還要復習一下兒語法。

A：回國以後你就研究中國現代文學嗎？

B：回國以後我還要念一年大學。

4. Coming across somebody whom one hasn't seen for a long time

A：很長時間沒見了，你去哪兒了？

B：我去天津 (Tiānjin Tianjin) 了，在那兒住了半個多月。

A：去那兒開會＊嗎？

B：不，我去看一個朋友，他身體不太好。

＊　　　　　＊　　　　　＊

六、語法 Grammar

1. The time-measure complement

A time-measure complement placed after a verb is employed to show the duration of an action or a state, e.g.

Noun or pronoun	Verb	Particle	Numeral-measure word indicating time	Particle
他 我 我們	休息 （每天）鍛鍊 （已經）分別	了	一天。 一個小時。 十年	了。

A verb with an object is generally repeated, and the verb may be followed at its second appearance by a time-measure complement if the sentence contains one.

Noun or pronoun	Verb	Noun or pronoun	Repeated verb	Particle	Numeral-measure word indicating time
我們 教練 她 哥哥	等 輔導 打 學	他 他們 電話 英文	等 輔導 打 學	了 了 了	二十分鐘。 兩個小時。 一刻鐘。 兩年。

If the object is a noun-personal pronoun, the time-measure complement (sometimes with " 的 ") may also be put between the verb and its object.

Noun or pronoun	Verb	Particle	Numeral-measure word indicating time	Particle "的"	Noun
我 他 古波 我	** 念 上 學 聽	了 了	四十分鐘 三小時 三年 一刻鐘	的 的	法文。 口語課。 中文。 新聞。

The object may be put before the subject of a sentence for emphasis or when the object has a very complicated structure, e.g.

那條裙子她找了一個多小時。

今天的報你要看一個晚上嗎?

這個很難的問題他想了兩天。

The former kind of word order normally does not apply to sentences containing a complicated object such as the sentences mentioned above. For example, it is wrong to say "她找了一個多小時的那條裙子。"

Note that when a sentence with a time-measure complement and an aspect particle "了" after its verb, contains a modal particle "了" at the end, the idea that the action is still continuing is suggested. E.g.

我們學習了兩年的中文了。 (It means the action "study" is still continuing.)

我們學習了兩年的中文。 (It does not tell whether the action "study" is still continuing or not.)

** 念 is interchangeable with 唸

2. The approximate number indicators " 幾 " and " 多 "

" 幾 " may be used to indicate an unspecific number smaller than ten as in " 幾個人(several people)", "十幾個小時 (ten-odd hours)" and " 幾十個學生 (some dozens of students)".

" 多 " as an approximate indicator of number, cannot stand alone, but must be used after an integer to show the remainder of the figure:

(1) " 多 " can be used after "十 " or "百 (bai, hundred)" as in " 十多本書 (ten-odd books)" and " 三百多年 (over three centuries)".

(2) " 多 " may be used between a measure word and a noun, or after a measure-noun, to express the remainder of a round figure, as in "三個多月 (over three months)", " 一個多小時 (a little over an hour)", "一年多 (one thousand odd)" and " 一天多 (a little longer than one day)".

七、練習 Exercises

1. Read aloud the following phrases:

(1) 第一次　第二天　第十二個
第二十九課

(2) 三個多小時　兩分多鐘　一刻多鐘
四個多星期　五個多月　兩年多
一天多
十多位老師　　二十多頂帽子
三十多個班　　五十多張紙
二十幾頂帽子　幾十個學生
幾瓶酒　　　　十幾位老師

(3) 吃飯的時候　這時候　有時候

什麼時候

多長時間　很多時間　有時間

什麼時間

(4) 為研究中國文學　為實現四個現代化為建設自己的國家

2. Complete the following sentences with verbs and time-measure complements:

(1) 昨天上午八點代表團開始參觀飛機工廠，十一點三十分
離開那兒，他們 ＿＿＿＿＿＿＿ 。

(2) 1937 年那位老華僑去美國，現在他還在那兒教書，他
已經 ＿＿＿＿＿＿＿ 。

(3) 她九點二十分開車，九點五十分到朋友家，她在路上
＿＿＿＿＿＿＿ 。

(4) 一九七九年十月他開始寫這本書，現在他已經 ＿＿＿＿＿ 。

(5) 帕蘭卡和古波去年到北京，明年回國，他們 ＿＿＿＿＿＿＿ 。

(6) 我弟弟每天晚上九點半睡覺，第二天六點起床，他每天
＿＿＿＿＿＿＿ 。

3. Use the following phrases to make sentences that contain a time-measure complement:

Example　吃飯

→ 他吃飯吃了二十分鐘。

(1) 談話　　(2) 滑冰　　(3) 照相

(4) 辦手續　(5) 找同學　(6) 洗澡

Example 聽音樂

→ 她聽了一刻鐘的音樂。

(1) 念課文 (2) 看球賽 (3) 學英語

(4) 看京劇 (5) 買東西 (6) 坐火車

4. Answer orally the following questions according to the timetable given and then write a short composition putting together all the answers:

　　　6：10 起床

　　　6：10—6：40 鍛鍊

　　　6：40—7：15 念課文

　　　7：15—7：35 吃早飯

　　　7：35—7：55 坐車去學校

　　　8：00—12：00 上課

　　12：00—12：30 吃午飯

　　12：30—2：00 休息

　　　2：00—3：00 聽錄音*

　　　3：00—4：00 看雜誌

　　　4：30—5：30 踢足球

　　　5：40—6：00 坐車回家

　　　6：00—6：30 吃晚飯

　　　7：30—9：30 復習

　　　9：30—10：00 聽新聞

　　10：30 睡覺

(1) 你每天幾點起床？起床以後鍛鍊多長時間？

(2) 你念課文嗎？你念多長時間的課文？

(3) 你幾點坐車去學校？路上坐車要坐多少分鐘？

(4) 你們上午上幾小時的課？

(5) 12 點半以後你作什麼？

(6) 下午你聽多長時間的錄音*？ 聽錄音*以後你還作什麼？

(7) 每天下午你都踢足球嗎？

(8) 你晚上幾點復習？ 你復習幾個小時？

(9) 晚上你還作什麼？

(10) 你每天睡幾個小時？

(11) 你已經學了多長時間的中文了？

(12) 第一本漢語書你學了幾個月？

5. Translate the following into Chinese:

   (1)   Last autumn the student returned from abroad for the first time.

   (2)   His visit began at two p.m. and lasted two hours.

   (3)   Every week we study for six days and have one day off.

   (4)   He sometimes watches TV for about half an hour in the evening or listens to news for 15 minutes or so.

   (5)   He has been translating this grammar book for more than two months.

   (6)   This summer I did not stay in Shanghai for long, I was there only a few days.

   (7)   The Chinese students study very hard abroad to prepare themselves for the country's four modernizations.

6. Make conversation about the pictures:

路上走了幾天？

在中國住多長時間？

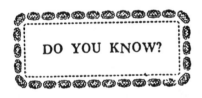

DO YOU KNOW?

Twelve Animal Names Used to Symbolize the Year of Birth

After telling you how old he is, a Chinese will sometimes add "I was born in the Horse year", or "I was born in the Hare year". The animal names "Horse" and "Hare" are used to symbolize the year in which a person is born.

There are two peculiar sets of serial numbers in China known as the Heavenly Stems and the Earthly Branches, which were used for centuries in the past to designate years, months and days. The Heavenly Stems are: "甲" (the first of the ten Heavenly Stems0),"乙, 丙, 丁, 戊, 己, 庚, 辛, 壬 and 癸" (indicating respectively the second, third, fourth, fifth,

(26,29)

sixth, seventh, eighth, ninth and tenth Heavenly Stems). The Earthly Branches are: " 子 " (the first of the Twelve Earthly Branches), " 丑, 寅, 卯, 辰, 巳, 午, 未, 申, 酉, 戌 and 亥 " (indicating the rest of the twelve Earthly Branches". The Ten Heavenly Stems combine with the Twelve Earthly Branches to form a sequential series of two-character phrases, and these are used to designate years, months and days. " 甲子 " (formed of the first of the Ten Heavenly Stems and the first of the Twelve Earthly Branches), " 乙丑 " are the first two of the sequential series. According to this way of designation, 1981 is the year of " 辛酉 ".

The Chinese traditionally associate the Twelve Earthly Branches also with twelve names of animals in a definite order to designate different years of birth. They are: 子鼠 (Rat), 丑牛 (Ox), 寅虎 (Tiger), 卯兔 (Hare), 辰龍 (Dragon), 巳蛇 (Snake), 午馬 (Horse), 未羊 (Sheep), 申猴 (Monkey), 酉鷄 (Cock), 戌狗 (Dog), 亥猪 (Pig)". According to this designating method, the year 1981 is the Cock year, and children born in 1981 are said to be born in the Cock year.

十二生肖

鼠 身靈巧性機伶　　馬 愛自由躍四方
牛 勤容忍負責任　　羊 跪求乳表孝思
虎 虎生威猛又強　　猴 怪頑皮赤子心
兔 喜和平心細膩　　鷄 鳴報曉展雄風
龍 行大運騰九空　　狗 重信義見忠貞
蛇 性冷靜穩又準　　猪 本樂天好福氣

第三十二課

一、課　文

你　最　近　透　視　過　沒　有

古　波：小張，醫務所在哪兒？

張華光：你去看病嗎？

古　波：不，我去檢查身體。我還沒去過醫務所呢。

張華光：跟我走吧。來北京一個多星期了，你們去過哪些地方
　　　　了？

古　波：去過長城和北海。

張華光：看過中國電影嗎？

古　波：在電視裡看過幾次電影。

張華光：今天晚上學校有電影，你去嗎？

古　波：什麼電影？

張華光：《大鬧天宮》。這個電影真不錯，我已經看過兩遍
　　　　了。

古　波：還想看第三遍嗎？今天晚上我們一起去吧。

(31,32)　　　　　　　　　　　　— 20 —

張華光：好。醫務所到了，你在那兒拿一張表，先到內科檢查。

古　波：大夫您好！

大　夫：你好，請坐。你第一次來中國嗎？

古　波：是啊。也是第一次來醫務所。

大　夫：你以前得過什麼病？

古　波：沒有。——對了，我小時候得過肺炎，病了兩個多星期。

大　夫：聽聽心臟，量一下兒血壓吧。……

古　波：大夫，我的心臟和血壓都正常嗎？

大　夫：都很正常，你最近透視過沒有？

古　波：去年二月透視過一次。

大　夫：時間太長了。請到對面房間透視一下兒吧。

古　波：透視以後就可以走了嗎？

大　夫：不，還要檢查一下兒眼睛、鼻子和耳朵。

古　波：我想這些都沒問題。

大　夫：我也希望這樣。

古　波：謝謝。我聽過這樣的話：爸爸媽媽給我生命，老師給我知識，大夫給我健康。

大　夫：這話很有意思。可是我希望你的健康不是大夫給的，要自己注意鍛鍊。祝你健康，再見！

二、生　詞

1. 最近	zuìjìn	recently; lately
2. 透視	tòushì	to examine by fluoroscope; to take X-ray examination
3. 過	guo	a particle
4. 醫務所	yīwùsuǒ	clinic
5. 看（病）	kàn(bìng)	to see (a doctor, etc.)
6. 病	bìng	to be ill; illness
7. 檢查	jiǎnchá	to have a check-up; check-up; a physical examination
8. 地方	dìfang	place
9. 遍	biàn	a measure word
10. 拿	ná	to get; to take
11. 表	biǎo	form (application form, etc.)
12. 先	xiān	first
13. 內科	nèikē	medical department
14. 以前	yǐqián	before; in the past
15. 得（病）	dé(bìng)	to fall ill; to contract a disease
16. 肺炎	fèiyán	pneumonia
肺	fèi	lungs

(34,35)　　　　　　　　　— 22 —

17.心臟	xīnzàng	heart
18.量	liáng	to measure
19.血壓	xuèyā	blood pressure
血	xuè	blood
20.正常	zhèngcháng	normal; regular
21.眼睛	yǎnjing	eye
22.鼻子	bízi	nose
23.耳朵	ěrduo	ear
24.這樣	zhèyàng	so; such; like this
25.生命	shēngmìng	life
26.知識	zhīshi	knowledge

專　　名

1.長城	Chángchéng	The Great Wall
2.北海	Běihǎi	Beihai Park
3.《大鬧天宮》	《Dànào-tiāngōng》	"The Monkey Creates Havoc in Heaven"

補　充　詞

1.肝	gān	liver
2.填	tián	to fill

3.胃	wèi	stomach
4.個子	gèzi	height; stature; build
5.頭髮	tóufa	hair (on the human head)
6.嘴	zuǐ	mouth

四、閱讀短文

一位留學生的作文**

　我是加拿大 (Jiānádà Canada) 留學生，以前沒來過中國，這是第一次。在加拿大我學過三年中文。開始的時候，我常常到一家華僑餐廳吃飯，認識了一位華僑朋友，他教我說中國話。我每星期還到中文系聽兩次課。我的朋友們常跟我說，中文非常難，讓我別學了。可是，我很喜歡中文。在學校裡，我認識了一些中國留學生，他們常常幫助我，所以我進步很快。學了兩年多的中文以後，我開始看中文畫報和雜誌，了解了一些中國的文化和歷史 (lìshǐ history)，我更喜歡中文了。我希望以後能研究中國醫學 (yīxué medical science) 。

　很早以前我就想到中國看看。現在能在中國學習，我非常高興。來北京快兩個星期了，我又認識了不少中國朋友。我的同屋 (tóngwū roommate) 是個中國同學，他的個子*不太大，身體很好，頭髮*和眼睛都很黑 (hēi dark)。他已經學了兩年的法語了。現在我們常常互相幫助，他是我的好朋友。

學校裡每星期有兩次中國電影。我已經看過三次了。今天晚上有一個新電影，我同屋說要跟我一起去看。

** 作文 Zuòwén, composition

四、注釋 Notes

1. "小張，醫務所在哪兒？"

"小張" is an intimate form of address for "張華光". It is common practice among Chinese to prefix the surname of a friend with "小" if he or she is very young, and with "老" if he or she is no longer young. When addressing close friends or members of the family such as the husband, wife, brothers, sisters or anybody of the younger generation, given names are used. "華光", for example, is customarily used for "張華光".

2. "來北京一個多星期了。"

"It's over a week since we came to Beijing."

Certain actions such as these expressed by "來，去，到，離開，下課" cannot be continued. To indicate a period of time from the occurrence of this kind of actions until the time of speaking, however, the time-measure complements may also be used and they are usually placed after the object of the sentence if the verbal predicate is followed by one, e.g.

他離開這兒已經一年多了。

下課已經五分鐘了，他們還在練習說漢語呢。

3. 《大鬧天宮》

"The Monkey Creates Havoc in Heaven" is a colour animated cartoon based on the mythological novel "Pilgrimage to the West" written in 16th century by the great Chinese writer Wu Chengen. The story describes how Xuan Zang, a monk of the Tang Dynasty, went on a pilgrimage to India for Buddhist scriptures. By using positive romanticist technique the author created the characters, the Monkey, Pigie and various others, who are known literally to everyone in China.

4. "還想看第三遍嗎？"

The adverb "還" (3), often found in an interrogative sentence or a sentence with an optative verb, may be used to indicate that the action referred to is going to take place once again. The adverb "還" generally comes before an optative verb which may at the same time be followed by "在". Here are two more examples:

這個電影你還看嗎?

我還想再看一遍。

5. "醫務所到了。"

"Here we are at the clinic."

6. "對了，我小時候得過肺炎。"

Here "對了" suggests that an idea has suddenly come to the speaker's mind. It is often used to correct or add some thing to what one has just stated.

"小時候" refers to one's childhood days.

7. "我想，這些都沒問題。"

"沒問題", meaning "normal" or "nothing has gone wrong" here, is used to indicate certainty or confidence, e.g.

明天你能來嗎?

沒問題，我一定來。

8. "可是，我希望你的健康不是大夫給的。"

"But I do hope you don't owe your health to your doctor."

五、替換與擴展 Substitution and Extension

(一)

1. 你知道《大鬧天宮》嗎?

我知道，我看過這個電影。

(38,39,40)

茅台酒，　　　　喝，茅台酒
魯迅，　　　　　看，他的書
老師的地址，　　去，他家
"有志者事竟成"，學，這個成語

2. 他看過京劇嗎？
他沒有看過京劇。

研究，語言
學，　古典文學
翻譯，這些生詞
走，　這條路
開，　車
拿，　這兒的報

3. 最近你去過北海嗎？
我去過。

得，　病
看，　內科
量，　血壓
看，　眼睛
檢查，肝*

4. 你以前訪問過那位老作家沒有?
   我訪問過那位老作家。
   你訪問過他幾次?
   我訪問過他兩次。

見,	那位華僑
找,	張大夫
問,	王老師
幫助,	你同學

5. 這課漢字你寫過幾遍了?
   我寫過兩遍了,我要再寫一遍。

課文(課),	念	
書(本),		看
歌兒(個),	聽	
電影(個),	看	

6. 他們請他作什麼?
   他們請他介紹一下兒長城。

回答,	那個問題
教,	游泳
唱,	那個民歌
停,	車
填*,	那張表

1. Offering greetings

   A：你爸爸最近身體怎麼樣?

   B：謝謝你，他心臟還不太好。

   A：血壓正常嗎?

   B：不知道，最近沒有量過。

            *   *   *

   A：你的胃*怎麼樣? 最近好點兒嗎?

   B：好點兒了，謝謝你。你檢查過鼻子嗎?

   A：檢查了，沒問題。

   B：那太好了。

2. Talking about personal experience or record

   A：我朋友格林 (Gélín) 先生很願意來你們學院工作。他
   希望在外語系工作一年。

   B：格林先生以前作過什麼工作?

   A：他在大學教過語言課，最近幾年在研究英語語法。
   對了，他還教過華僑學生英語。

   B：謝謝您的介紹，我們再研究 (yánjiū to discuss; to consi-
   der) 一下兒，以後告訴您。

            *   *   *

   A：你看過《家》這本書嗎?

   B：看過。這是中國有名的作家巴金 (Bā Jīn) 先生寫的。

   A：這本書太好了。我以前看過一遍，現在我研究中國
   現代文學，想再看一遍。

3. Talking about a past happening

A：你去哪兒了？

B：我進城了。有事兒嗎？

A：張華光來找過你兩次，你都不在。

B：啊，真糟糕 (zāogāo what bad luck)！星期三我給他打過電話，讓他今天來，可是我忘了這事兒了。

*　　　*　　　*

六、語法　Grammar

1. The aspect particle "過" indicating experience

The aspect particle "過" which occurs immediately after a verb denotes that some action took place in the past. It is often used to emphasize experience. Here are some more examples:

他去過日本。

我小時候學過一點兒法文，現在都忘了。

這個字應該這樣寫，老師教過我們。

我朋友足球踢得很好，他參加過比賽。

The negative form of "過" is "沒 (有)…過", e.g.

我沒有看過那個電影。

— 31 —

(44,46,47)

這本詞典很新，還沒有用過。

他走了以後沒給我來過信。

帕蘭卡沒離開過媽媽。

The affirmative-negative question with "過" is "…過…沒有", e.g.

你檢查過身體沒有？

你以前跳過舞沒有？

這個成語你學過沒有？

Points to be noted:

(1) "過" should be placed immediately after the verb. If the verbal predicate has an object, "過" always precedes the object. It is therefore wrong, for example, to say "我檢查身體過".

(2) To indicate one's past experience. "過" is normally placed after the second verb in a sentence with verbal constructions in series, e.g.

他去醫務所量過血壓。

我用法文寫過信。

2. The action-measure complement

The action-measure word "次" or "遍" etc. often goes with a numeral and is used after the verb as an action-measure complement, to show the frequency of an action. In addition to signifying the number of times, "遍" also indicates the whole process of an action from beginning to end, e.g.

我去年透視過一次。

今天的練習我又檢查了兩遍。

When the object is expressed by a noun, the action-measure comple-ment should be placed before the object. When it is expressed by a pronoun, the complement often comes after the object.

Noun or pronoun	Verb	Particle	Pronoun	Numeral plus action-measure word	Noun
他 我們 我 大夫	量 聽 找 來	過 了 過 過	他 這兒	一次 一遍 幾次。 兩次。	血壓。 新聞。

Apart from showing explicit frequency of an action, the complement "一下兒" is also used to indicate an action done in a casual way or lasting for only a little while. Its function is similar to a repeated verb. E.g.

我給你們介紹一下兒。

要量一下兒血壓嗎?

請你幫助我一下兒。

七、練習 Exercises

1. Read aloud the following phrases:

    (1) 這樣寫　　　這樣翻譯　這樣唱

        這樣的學生　這樣的病　這樣的知識

　　　　　　　　　　(48,49,50)

(2) 檢查身體　檢查眼睛　檢查行李
　　檢查漢字　檢查課文　檢查練習

(3) 到過長城　來過中國　看過內科
　　得過很多病　　見過那位老先生
　　訪問過老華僑　打過一次電話
　　告訴過他幾遍　輔導過他一次
　　開過五年車　　聽過很多遍
　　參加過一次招待會

2. Give negative answers to the following questions, then change them into affirmative-negative questions:

Example　你研究過民歌嗎?

　　　　→我沒研究過民歌。

　　　　你研究過民歌沒有?

(1) 他得過肺炎嗎?

(2) 你檢查過心臟嗎?

(3) 你訪問過那位老華僑嗎?

(4) 古波拿過那本中國畫報嗎?

(5) 你聽過王老師的語法課嗎?

(6) 大夫的話你告訴過他嗎?

(7) 他給你回過信嗎?

(8) 北京隊贏過國家隊嗎?

3. Fill in the blanks with the words "次", "遍" or "下兒":

(1) 請你再說一 ＿＿＿＿。

(2) 大夫說我的血壓不正常，明天還要來量一 ＿＿＿＿。

(3) 今天的漢字老師讓我們寫兩_____。

(4) 他最近進了兩_____城。

(5) 這個問題很難，請讓我想一_____。

(6) 我現在沒有時間，你能等一_____嗎?

(7) 他們跟工人隊比賽，贏過一_____，也輸過一_____。

4. Make up dialogues with the following phrases and then write the dialogues down:

   (1) 去過　參觀過　訪問過　看過　了解過

   (2) 得過　檢查過　聽過　量過

5. Playing games in groups:

   A says the names of the following parts of the body. B must promptly indicate by the use of his finger that part of the body. If a mistake is made or if the reaction is slow, then a minus or negative point is scored.

   鼻子　眼睛
   耳朵　嘴*

第三十三課

一、課　文

現在下雨了

帕蘭卡：四點多了，李老師不來了吧？

古　波：聽，有人敲門，李老師來了。

李老師：古波在嗎？

古　波：在，請進。

李老師：啊，帕蘭卡也在這兒。你們好！

帕蘭卡：您好，請坐。李老師，請您喝杯咖啡吧？

李老師：謝謝。今天天氣很好，你們沒到公園玩兒玩兒嗎？

古　波：上午去頤和園了。

李老師：香山去過嗎？

帕蘭卡：還沒去過。那兒怎麼樣？

李老師：香山的紅葉很漂亮。現在是秋天了，樹上的葉子都紅了，可以看紅葉了。

古　波：我們一定去。以前有人告訴我，北京夏天很熱，到北京以後，我覺得不太熱。

李老師：這幾年天氣不正常。你知道嗎？北京的秋天天氣最好，可是今年秋天也常常下雨。你們看，今天上午是晴天，現在下雨了。

古　波：北京冬天冷不冷？

李老師：冬天很冷，常常颳風、下雪。

帕蘭卡：在中國冬天有什麼花兒？

李老師：很多地方有梅花。在大風大雪的天氣，梅花不怕風，不怕雪，開得很好，所以大家都喜歡梅花。從古時候到今天，文學家為梅花寫了不少詩。

古　波：您教我們一首，好嗎？

李老師：這樣的詩很多。我給你們念一首吧，是陳毅的《紅梅》：

　　　　隆冬到來時，百花迹已絕。

　　　　紅梅不屈服，樹樹立風雪。

帕蘭卡：這首詩真好，請您再介紹一首。

李老師：時間不早了，雨也停了，我們以後再介紹吧。古波，這是你要的那本語法書。

古　波：謝謝您。您再坐坐吧。

李老師：不坐了，我還有點事兒，再見！

帕蘭卡：希望您常來，再見！

二、生　詞

1. 下（雨）	xià(yǔ)	to rain
2. 雨	yǔ	rain
3. 敲	qiāo	to knock (at a door)
4. 公園	gōngyuán	park
5. 紅葉	hóngyè	red autumnal leaves (of the maple, etc.)
6. 樹	shù	tree
7. 葉子	yèzi	leaf
8. 熱	rè	hot
9. 覺得	juéde	to think; to feel
10. 最	zuì	best; most; least; to the highest (lowest) degree
11. 晴	qíng	(of weather) fine; bright; clear
12. 冷	lěng	cold
13. 颳（風）	guā(fēng)	to blow (said of wind)
14. 風	fēng	wind
15. 雪	xuě	snow
16. 梅花	méihuā	plum blossom
17. 怕	pà	to be afraid; to fear
18. 開（花兒）	kāi(huār)	(of flowers) to open out; blossom

(60,61)

19. 古	gǔ	ancient
20. 詩	shī	poem; poetry; verse
21. 首	shǒu	a measure word
22. 隆冬	lóngdōng	midwinter; the depth of winter
23. 百	bǎi	hundred
24. 迹	jī	trace; track; sign
25. 絕	jué	to disappear; to vanish; absolutely
26. 屈服	qūfú	to surrender; to yield
27. 立	lì	to stand; to erect

專　　名

1. 頤和園	Yíhéyuán	Summer Palace
2. 香山	Xiāngshān	Fragrance Hill (Park)
3. 陳毅	Chén Yì	name of a person

補　充　詞

1. 霧	wù	fog; mist
2. 涼快	liángkuai	nice and cold; pleasantly cool
3. 春天	chūntiān	spring
4. 預報	yùbào	forecast
5. 陰天	yīntiān	cloudy day; overcast sky

6. 度	dù	a measure word, degree
7. 習慣	xíguàn	to be used to; to be accustomed to; habit; custom
8. 暖和	nuǎnhuo	warm; nice and warm

三、閱讀短文

北 京 的 天 氣

北京一年有四個季節(jìjié season)：春天、夏天、秋天和冬天。

北京的冬天時間最長。冬天天氣很冷，常常颳風，有時候下雪。最冷的時候到過零(líng zero) 下二十二度*。第一年帕蘭卡很不習慣*，得過一次感冒(gǎnmào cold) 。北京人很喜歡滑冰，冬天在北海滑冰很有意思。

北京的春天很暖和*。這時候樹綠了，花兒開了，公園裡人也多了。春天時間不太長，這兒很少下雨，有時候颳大風。

從六月到八月是北京的夏天，夏天天氣不太熱。最熱的時候是七月，七月、八月常常下雨。夏天的頤和園是大家常去的地方，很多人去那兒游泳、釣魚。

九月，北京的秋天到了。秋天是北京最好的季節，天天都是晴天，不冷也不熱，非常涼快*。十一月到了，香山的樹葉都紅了，大家都喜歡去看紅葉。很多外國朋友都在這時候到北京來參觀。

(62,69,70)

四、注釋　Notes

1. "這幾年天氣不正常。"

"這幾年" means "in the past few years". Similarly we can say "這幾天 (these days)", "這幾個月 (these months)" and "這幾個星期(these weeks)" etc.

2. "北京的秋天天氣最好。"

The adverb "最" may be used before an adjective or a verb to express the superlative degree.

3. "我給你們念一首吧，是陳毅的《紅梅》。"

Marshal Chen Yi (1901—1972), a native of Lezhi County, Sichuan Province, was the former Vice Premier and Foreign Minister of the People's Republic of China. He was not only a statesman, strategist and diplomat, but also a well-known poet. His works of poetry include "Chen Yi's Poems in Manuscript" and "Selected Poems of Chen Yi".

4. "隆冬到來時"

"when the severe winter comes"

"到來" means "to arrive".

5. "百花迹已絕"

"Flowers have vanished from sight."

"已" means the same as "已經" used mainly in written language.

6. "紅梅不屈服"

"The red plum blossoms do not yield to frigidity."

7. "樹樹立風雪"

"Every tree stands firm, braving snowstorms."

Here "樹樹" means "every tree". When a measure word or a noun such as "人", "年" and "天" is repeated, the idea of "each" or "every" is conveyed. Hence "個個" is equivalent to "每個(each)", "本本" means "每本 (each copy)", "人人" means "每人 (everyone)" and "家家" means "每家 (every household)".

五、替換與擴展 Substitution and Extension

(一)

1. 颳風了嗎?
   是啊，我來的時候天氣很
   好，現在颳風了。

下雨
下雪
下霧*

2. 雨小了嗎?
   沒有，雨還很大。

風，	大，	很小
雪，	停，	很大
葉子，	紅，	很綠
天氣，	涼快*，	很熱
他的病，	好，	不太好
這間屋子，	舊，	很新

3. 你去過香山嗎?
   沒有。
   現在是秋天了，可以去香山看紅葉了。

北海，	冬天，	滑冰
頤和園，	夏天，	游泳
那個公園，	春天*，	看花

4. 現在幾點了?

十一點了,(應)該睡覺了。

六點半,　　起床
七點五十五,上課
九點多,　　出發
十二點一刻,吃飯
五點,　　　休息

5. 他告訴我,他今天要
去學校。
不,他有事兒,他不
去了。

檢查,身體
量,　血壓
參加,球賽
輔導,你們

6. 李老師在嗎?
在。什麼事兒?
有人找您。
好,我就來。

敲,　門
來看,您
在等,您
問,問題

— 43 —

(65,66)

7. 下午你們從幾點到幾點上課?

我們從兩點到三點上課。

```
工作，  1：30,  5：30
鍛鍊，  5：00,  6：00
參觀，  1：00,  4：30
賽球，  3：00,  5：00
```

（二）

Talking about the weather

A：今天天氣真好。我希望星期天也是晴天。

B：天氣預報*說明天是陰天，星期天要下雪。

A：是嗎? 星期天我們不能去頤和園了。

B：下雪的時候，頤和園更漂亮。你應該去照幾張相。

　　　　　*　　　　*　　　　*

A：今天真冷。

B：是啊，零 (líng zero) 下十度*了。明天怎麼樣? 你聽天氣預報*了嗎?

A：明天要颳大風了。

B：那就會更冷。你要多穿點兒，注意身體。

A：謝謝你。

　　　　　*　　　　*　　　　*

A：不下雨了吧?

B：還在下呢。你再坐一會兒＊吧。

A：四點鐘有人找我，現在已經三點半了，我該走了。

B：再等一等，……你看，現在雨小了，快要停了。

＊　　　＊　　　＊

A：這兒的夏天你習慣＊嗎?

B：開始我覺得太熱，現在已經習慣＊了。

A：你們那兒天氣怎麼樣?

B：我們那兒夏天不太熱，最熱的時候三十度＊。

A：冬天冷不冷?

B：冬天很冷。

A：常常下雪嗎?

B：常下雪。可是去年天氣很不正常，冬天沒有下過雪。

＊　　　＊　　　＊

六、語法　Grammar

1. The subjectless sentence

The great majority of Chinese sentences are composed of two parts: the subject and the predicate. However there are a few types of sentences

— 45 —

that have no subjects. The following two are the most common:

(1)   Subjectless sentences for describing natural phenomena, e.g.

要颳風了。

下雨呢。

(2)   Subjectless pivotal sentences beginning with "有", e.g.

有人請他看京劇。

聽，有人在唱歌兒。

上午有兩個人來找你。

有人給他打了一個電話。

2.   The modal particle "了" (3)

In sentences with an adjectival predicate, the modal particle "了" may indicate changed circumstances, e.g.

現在天氣冷了。　（以前不冷）

最近我不太忙了。　（以前很忙）

樹上的葉子都紅了。　（以前不紅）

雨大了。　（以前不大）

In sentences with a nominal predicate, "了" is also employed to show that some new circumstances have emerged, e.g.

現在四點了，我們去鍛鍊吧。

她今年二十一（歲）了。

In sentences with a verbal predicate, "了" may either confirm that something has occurred or some circumstances have emerged. Sometimes this modal particle also indicates changed circumstances. Here are some more examples:

他現在是大學生了。（以前不是大學生）

我明天不去學校了。（原來想去學校）

我弟弟會游泳了。（以前不會）

他有工作了。（以前沒有）

3. The construction "從…到…"

In the construction "從…到…", "從" and "到" may be followed either by words indicating location or by words indicating time to express the distance of time and space, e.g.

從這兒到醫務所不太遠。

他從 1977 年到 1979 年在北京大學學習。

七、練習 Exercises

1. Read aloud the following phrases:

(1) 颳大風　下大雨　下大雪　下小雨
　　有大風　有大雨　有大雪　有小雨
　　有風　　有小雪

(2) 很熱　　很長　　很怕
　　很希望　很注意　很辛苦
　　更熱　　更長　　更怕
　　更希望　更注意　更辛苦
　　最熱　　最長　　最怕
　　最希望　最注意　最辛苦

(3) 覺得冷　　覺得遠　　覺得很忙

　　覺得難　　覺得很對　　覺得很好看

2. Complete the following sentences:

(1) 車來了，＿＿＿＿＿＿＿。

(2) 上課了，＿＿＿＿＿＿＿。

(3) 時間到了，＿＿＿＿＿＿＿。

(4) 休息了，＿＿＿＿＿＿＿。

(5) 吃飯了，＿＿＿＿＿＿＿。

(6) 已經十一點了，＿＿＿＿＿＿＿。

(7) 下雪了，＿＿＿＿＿＿＿。

(8) 晴天了，＿＿＿＿＿＿＿。

3. Answer the following questions on the text:

(1) 帕蘭卡請李老師喝什麼了？

(2) 秋天的時候，香山公園怎麼樣？

(3) 北京最好的天氣是什麼時候？

(4) 為什麼大家都很喜歡梅花？

(5) 你能給大家介紹一下兒陳毅的《紅梅》詩嗎？

4. Translate the following into Chinese using the words in the brackets:

(1) It was fine when I left home.　But now it has become windy and it's going to rain.（了）

(2) Someone told me that there were plum blossoms everywhere in China, and that they were very nice to look at.（有人）

(3) It is getting warm enough for people to go swimming. Would you like to go for a dip?（了）

(4) I'll have a busy afternoon today, for a friend of mine is coming to see me.（有一個朋友）

(5) It has been quite windy these days. （天天）

(6) He doesn't mind cold weather, but he can't stand heat. （怕）

(7) He used to work as an interpreter, but now he is a teacher. （了）

(8) I feel summer is the best season here. （覺得）

(9) May I keep this book for another week? （再）

(10) His illness prevented him from coming to the school since last Monday. （從星期一到今天）

5. Fill in the brackets under the picture with proper sentences:

外邊下雨呢　下雨了　雨大了

要下雨了　不下了

(　　) (　　)

(　　) (　　) (　　)

6. Say something about the weather in your country.

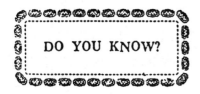
China's Climate

China extends over 5,500 kilometers from north to south and crosses 49 degrees of latitude over the frigid, temperate and subtropical zones. Over 90 percent of the land, however, is in the temperate zone. If you travel north in January from Guangzhou (Canton) you will go through a range of climates all in one day. When you start out, the temperature will be around 13.2 C. At Wuhan the temperature will drop to about 3.9 C. At Beijing, the temperature can be 4.6 C below zero and at Ha'erbin in the northeast as low as 20.9 C below zero. From Guangzhou, where you can just wear a lined jacket to keep you warm, to Ha'erbin, where fur clothes will be necessary, the temperature shows a difference of 30 degrees Celsius.

城市	廣州	福州	昆明	重慶	漢口	杭州	上海	南京	青島	北平	開封	西安	潘陽	蘭州
天氣	陣雨	陣雨	多雲	晴天	多雲	雨天	雨天	雨天	多雲	多雲	晴天	晴天	晴天	多雲
最高温	卅四度	卅二度		卅九度	卅八度	卅八度	卅五度		廿九度	廿八度	廿七度	廿六度	廿七度	
最低温	廿六度	廿五度	十八度	廿四度	廿五度	廿四度	廿四度		廿五度	廿四度	廿二度	廿二度	十七度	

第三十四課

一、課　文

圖片上寫著："怎樣寫信封？"

下了一上午的雨，下午天晴了。

帕蘭卡跟丁雲分別的時候，丁雲跟她説過：到北京以後一定要去家裡看看。今天，她給丁雲的媽媽寫了一封信，問他們什麼時間有空兒，她想去看他們。古波也要給南京的朋友寄一封信，他們一起去郵局。

六點多了，郵局的門還開著呢。郵局裡人很多，有的坐著寫信，有的等著寄東西。他們到了一個窗口前邊。那兒掛著一個牌子，牌子上寫著"郵票●掛號"；櫃檯裡放著很多漂亮的郵票和明信片。帕蘭卡跟營業員説："同志，我想買幾張明信片。"營業員熱情地回答："有，這兒有介紹北京的。請看，天安門、北海、頤和園、香山……。我想您一定很喜歡。"帕蘭卡笑著説："對，就要這些。我想讓家裡人也看看北京。"

古波拿著他的信跟營業員説："我要寄航空掛號信。"營業員看了看信封說："寄本市的信沒有航空的。"古波大聲地說："不，這不是寄本市的，是寄南京的。"營業員又看了看古波的信封，她笑了；帕蘭卡一看，也笑了。她們為什麼笑呢？古波的信封，上邊寫著他自己的地址和姓名，下邊寫著收信人的地址、姓名。營業員指著牆上的圖片說："中文的信封應該這樣寫。"古波一看，圖片上寫著："怎樣寫信封？"……

二、生　詞

1. 圖片	túpiàn	picture; photograph
2. 著**	zhe	a particle
3. 信封	xìnfēng	envelope
4. 封	fēng	a measure word
5. 寄	jì	to post; to mail
6. 郵局	yóujú	post office
7. 有的	yǒude	some
8. 窗口	chuāngkǒu	window
9. 掛	guà	to hang; to put up
10. 牌子	páizi	sign; plate
11. 郵票	yóupiào	stamp
12. 掛號	guà hào	to register (a letter, etc.)
13. 櫃檯	guìtái	counter

** 着 is interchangeable with 著

(81,82)

— 52 —

14. 放	fàng	to put; to place
15. 明信片	míngxìnpiàn	postcard
16. 營業員	yíngyèyuán	clerk; shop assistant
營業	yíngyè	to do business
17. 地	de	a particle
18. 航空	hángkōng	air (mail)
19. 本	běn	this ; one's own; native
20. 市	shì	city
21. 大聲	dàshēng	loud voice; (read, speak, etc.) loudly
22. 為什麼	wèi shénme	why
23. 姓名	xìngmíng	full name; surname and given name
24. 下邊	xiàbiān	below; under; underneath
25. 收	shōu	to receive
26. 指	zhǐ	to point at; to point to
27. 牆	qiáng	wall

專　名

1. 南京	Nánjīng	Nanjing (city)
2. 天安門	Tiān'ānmén	Tiananmen (Gate of Heavenly Peace)

補　充　詞

1.燈	dēng	lamp; light
2.收音機	shōuyīnjī	radio
3.信箱	xìnxiāng	post-office box (P. O. B.); letter box; mail box
4.平信	píngxìn	ordinary mail
5.收據	shōujù	receipt
6.包裹	bāoguǒ	parcel
7.單	dān	bill; list; form
8.電報	diànbào	telegram; cable

三、閱讀短文

士 兵 和 將 軍

古時候有一年冬天，天氣非常冷。一天晚上，颳著大風，下著大雪。路上已經沒有人了，可是有一個士兵(shìbīng soldier)正在外邊站崗(zhàn gǎng to stand sentry)。從下午到現在他還沒有吃一點兒東西。他穿得不多，在風雪裡站著，覺得非常冷。

這時候，就在離他不遠的客廳裡，將軍(jiāngjūn army general)正在喝酒呢。客廳裡生著火(shēng zhe huǒ to light a fire)，將軍喝了很多酒，覺得非常熱。他很不高興地說：“已經十二月了，應該冷了，可是現在還這樣熱，天氣真不正常！”

在外邊站崗的士兵一聽，大聲地說：“將軍，您那兒的天

氣不正常，您很不高興，可是我覺得這兒的天氣很正常。您喜
歡正常的天氣，請您也到外邊站一站吧。"

四、注釋 Notes

1. "怎樣寫信封?"

"怎樣", meaning as "怎麼樣" here, is mostly used in written Chinese.

2. "就要這些。"

Here "就" (3) is employed to signify emphatic confirmation, that what is stated is true. E.g. "這就是天安門。"

3. "我想讓家裏人也看看北京。"

"家裏人" refers to the members of one's own family.

4. "我要寄航空掛號信。"

"I want to send this letter by registered air mail."

5. "寄本市的信沒有航空的。"

"Local letters don't go by air mail."

6. "帕蘭卡一看，也笑了。"

"When Palanka looked at it, she laughed too."

When "一" comes before some verbs, it indicates that when an action takes place, something immediately results or some state immediately results or some state immediately emerges. E.g. "我一看，雨已經停了。"

7. "下邊寫著收信人的地址、姓名。"

"收信人" means addressee and "寄信人" sender.

五、替換與擴展 Substitution and Extension

(一)

1. 他拿著什麼?
   他拿著一封信。

穿，	新襯衫
指，	一張圖片
看，	花兒
敲，	桌子

(84,85)

— 56 —

2. 學校的門開著沒有?
　　學校的門沒開著。

車門　　　　　　客廳裏的電視
厨房裏的燈 * 房間裏的收音機*

3. 窗口前邊掛著什麼?
　　窗口前邊掛著一個牌子。

櫃檯裏，放，很多信封
桌子上，放，酒和菜
箱子裏，放，幾件襯衫
客廳裏，掛，一張照片
牆上，　掛，中國地圖
床下，　放，一雙鞋

4. 圖片上寫著漢字沒有?
　　圖片上沒有寫著漢字，寫著英文。

那張明信片　信封
那個牌子　　本子

5. 他們在作什麼呢?

   他們<u>坐著</u><u>寫信</u>呢。

笑著，	談話
站著，	打電話
等著，	買電影票
看著書，	回答問題
喝著咖啡，	聽音樂

6. 郵局裏人多不多?

   郵局裏人很多，有的<u>坐著寫信</u>，有的<u>等著寄東西</u>。

閱覽室，	站著找畫報，	坐著看雜誌
食堂，	坐著吃飯，	站著買菜
公園，	在游泳，	在釣魚
醫務所，	在看病，	在檢查身體

(二)

1. Posting a letter

   A : 請問，哪兒有信箱 * ?

   B : 看，對面銀行旁邊掛著一個。

   A : 謝謝你。

   　　　　*　　　*　　　*

   A : 請問，到埃及(Āijí Egypt) 的信要多少天?

   B : 你寄平信 * 還是寄航空信?

A：航空信。

B：要一個星期。

A：我要掛號。

......

B：這是掛號收據*，請收好。

2. Sending a parcel by post

A：同志，我要寄一個包裹*。

B：裏面裝　(zhuāng to hold) 著什麼?

A：一頂帽子和兩條裙子。

B：這是包裹單*，您到那兒坐著寫吧。

A：好。

3. Sending a telegram

A：請問，打國際電報*在幾號窗口?

B：在五號窗口。

......

A：同志，請給我一張電報*紙。

謝謝。可以打英文電報嗎?

C：可以，請寫得清楚(qīngchu clear) 點兒。

A：您看，這樣可以嗎?

C：下邊還要寫您的姓名和地址。

A：啊，我忘了。

*　　　*　　　*

(87,88,89)

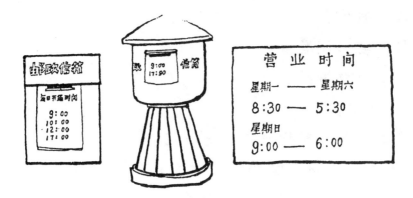

六、語法　Grammar

1.　The continuous aspect of an action:

The aspect particle "著" when occurring after a verb, indicates the continuation of the action, e.g.

孩子們都在椅子上坐著。

他拿著一張表去找大夫。

牆上掛著幾張照片。

牌子上寫著 " 請不要吸煙 " 。

The negative form of this sentence pattern is "沒（有）…著 ", e.g.

這個信封上沒有寫著寄信人的名字。

他寫漢字的時候，沒看著書。

In an affirmative-negative interrogative sentence "…著…沒有" is used, e.g.

電視開著沒有?

樓上住著人沒有?

The first verb or verbal structure in a sentence with verbal constructions in series may take the aspect particle "著" to indicate the manner in which the action expressed by the verb after it takes place or is performed.

Noun or pronoun	Verb (1)	Aspect particle "著"	Noun or pronoun	Verb (2)	Noun or pronoun
他	開	著	車	去	香山。
學生們	看	著	課文	回答	問題。
他朋友	穿	著	新裙子	參加	招待會。

Points to be noted:

(1) The continuation of an action generally implies that the action is in progress. For this reason, "著" often goes with words like "正在", "正", "在" or "呢", e.g.

郵局的門還開著呢。

他敲門的時候，我正打著電話呢。

外邊下著雨呢。

(2) Verbs with "著" do not take complements. (It is incorrect, for example, to say "他寫著漢字寫十分鐘。")

2. The structural particle "地"

When a dissyllabic or polysyllabic adjective modifies a verb adverbially, it is generally followed by the structural particle "地", e.g.

他高興地說："這個問題我懂了。"

這個工廠的工人為了實現四個現代化努力地工作。

(91,92,93)

上課的時候古波注意地聽，下課以後他認真地復習。

Note that an adjective may serve either as a complement to a verb or an adverbial modifier. The two uses are thus quite different:

(1)　A complement of degree is generally used to refer to the action itself, while an adverbial modifier describes how the doer acts, e.g.

他漢語聽得不多，他應該多聽漢語。

古波復習課文復習得很認真，我也要認真地復習。

(2)　A complement of degree is used mostly in connexion with an action that has already taken place or that frequently occurs; an adverbial modifier on the other hand may denote an action that has not yet happened. E.g.

他每天都來得很晚。老師讓他明天早點兒來。

我以前學過游泳，但是游得不好。今年夏天可以很好地學一學。

3.　The construction "有的…有的…"

When the pronoun "有的" is used as an adjective modifier, it refers to only part of what is indicated by the noun that it modifies. It may occur once, twice or three times, in a sentence, e.g.

有的字我還不知道怎麼樣寫。

有的櫃檯裏放着裙子，有的櫃檯裏放着襯衫。

我們班有（的）人喜歡看京劇，有（的）人喜歡看電影，有（的）人喜歡聽音樂。

In the above example, the word "的", in "有的人" may be omitted.

** 着 is interchangeable with 著

If the noun modified by "有的" has appeared previously, it may be omitted, e.g.

小張的郵票很多，有的是中國的，有的是外國的。

Note that generally speaking, a noun modified by "有的" cannot be placed after a verb. Instead of "我不喜歡有的民歌", we should say "有的民歌我不喜歡".

七、練習　Exercises

1. Read aloud the following phrases:

    (1) 坐著寫　站著看　笑著說　走著去

    (2) 指著那兒問　看著圖片說

    　　喝著咖啡談　拿著行李去

    (3) 注意地聽　大聲地唱　認真地研究

    　　難過地說　高興地問　熱情地回答

2. Fill in each of the blanks with a proper verb plus the particle "著":

    (1) 那邊牆上＿＿＿＿什麼？

    (2) 車上沒＿＿＿＿葡萄酒。

    (3) 宿舍的門＿＿＿＿呢，他不在裏邊，去哪兒了？

    (4) 帕蘭卡＿＿＿＿一束鮮花去看朋友。

    (5) 她今天＿＿＿＿一件綠襯衫。

    (6) 李老師喜歡＿＿＿＿給我們上課。

    (7) 古波＿＿＿＿說："我要那張郵票。"

    (8) 在大風大雪的天氣，梅花還＿＿＿＿。

－ 63 －

3. Fill in the blanks with "有的…":

    (1) 客廳裏 _____ 坐著喝茶，_____ 站著談話。

    (2) 桌子上的書很多，_____ 是中文的，_____ 是英文的。

    (3) 我們班下午去參觀，可是 _____ 不想去。

    (4) 我們星期天常去外邊玩兒，_____ 去天安門，_____ 去頤和園。

4. Translate the following sentences into Chinese:

    (1) Whenever I go to the post office, the clerk always attends to me in a most cordial manner. （熱情地）

    (2) The child cried and said, "I don't want to go to school." （哭著）

    (3) Do you know how to use chopsticks? （怎麼樣）

    (4) There are a lot of people queueing up before the counter in the bank. （站著）

    (5) Having checked him carefully, the doctor said with a smile, "Your heart and blood pressure are both normal." （笑著）

    (6) He felt it was a nice song as soon as he heard it. （一聽）

    (7) Look, the character should be written like this. （這樣）

    (8) Why are you so fond of plum blossoms? （為什麼）

5. Retell the following joke:

    有一個小姑娘到郵局寄信。營業員說："你的信太重 (zhòng heavy) 了，應該再貼 (tiē to stick) 一張郵票。"小姑娘驚奇 (jīngqí in surprise) 地問："為什麼？再貼一張郵票，信就更重了！"

6. Make questions about the following pictures and then answer them:

7. Read the following passage, then write a description of your own room giving the actual facts. Try to use the particle "着" whenever you can.

這個房間住著我一個人，是我的臥室，也是我的書房。

房間裏邊放著一張床，床對面的牆上掛著一張中國畫兒 (huàr painting)，上邊畫著梅花，旁邊還寫著陳毅的《紅梅》詩。

我的窗戶 (chuānghu window) 前邊放著一張桌子，兩把 (bǎ a measure word) 椅子。桌子上邊放著我常看的書和一個小電視。上午，我喜歡在窗戶前邊站著唸課文**，晚上我在椅子上坐著看電視。

這個房間不大，可是我覺得很好。

** 念 is interchangeable with 唸

(98, 99)

第三十五課

復　習

一、課　文

談　學　習

　　時間過得真快，古波和帕蘭卡到北京快一個月了。帕蘭卡怕媽媽不放心，已經給家裡寫過三次信，還寄了一些照片。媽媽也給她來過兩封信。

　　到北京語言學院的第三天，他們就參加了一次考試。這次考試，有的同學考得非常好，有的差一點兒。他們倆的成績都不錯。李老師說，他們先在語言學院學習一學期漢語，以後再到北京大學學習專業。

　　古波總覺得自己的口語不太好，這半年要更多地練習聽和說。現在，他每天下午都跟他的好朋友張華光說一個小時的漢語。小張是外語系英語專業的學生，他在這兒已經學了一年多了。他進步很快，現在可以跟古波用英語談話了。今天，他問古波："你在你們國家學習中文的時候，怎麼樣練習口語呢？

(102,103)

－ 66 －

”古波說：“來中國以前，我說中國話的機會也很少。有一個中國留學生叫丁雲，她非常熱情地幫助我們。上課的時候，中國老師總是讓我們多說、多念。可是你知道，每學期我們上課的時間不太多。夏天到了放暑假；冬天來了放寒假。在假期裡我沒有時間復習。”小張一聽，覺得很奇怪：“你們的假期很長，為什麼不能復習復習學過的東西呢？”古波笑著回答：“你沒到過我們國家，不了解那兒的情況。我們的暑假很長，可是我常常利用假期工作，掙點兒錢，開學以後用。現在好了，在這兒說漢語的機會多了，以後我們互相幫助吧。”

古波和小張正在宿舍裡談著話，帕蘭卡來了。她著急地問：“已經六點多了，你們還坐著說話，不吃飯了嗎？”古波一看錶，啊，真太晚了。他們一起去食堂吃飯。

二、生　詞

1.考試	kǎoshì	to test; examination
考	kǎo	to test
2.成績	chéngjì	result; achievement
3.學期	xuéqī	term; semester
4.專業	zhuānyè	speciality; specialized subject
5.機會	jīhuì	chance; opportunity
6.放（假）	fàng(jià)	to have a holiday or vacation

7. 暑假	shǔjià	summer vacation
8. 寒假	hánjià	winter vacation
9. 假期	jiàqī	vacation
10. 奇怪	qíguài	surprised
11. 情況	qíngkuàng	condition; situation; state of affairs
12. 利用	lìyòng	to use; to make use of
13. 掙	zhèng	to earn; to make (money)
14. 錢	qián	money
15. 開學	kāi xué	school opens; new term begins
16. 著急	zhāo jí	feel anxious, worried
17. 錶	biǎo	(wrist) watch

談學習

1. "古波和帕蘭卡到北京快一個月了。"

"It'll soon be a month since Gubo and Palanka came to Beijing."

2. "到北京語言學院的第三天。"

"on the third day after they entered the Beijing Languages Institute"

3. "他們先在語言學院學習一學期漢語，以後再到北京大學學習專業。"

The adverb "再" (2) may be used to indicate that an action occurs after the conclusion of another action (the adverb "先" is sometimes placed before the foregoing verb), or after a specific event or a given point of time. E.g. "雨停了你再走吧。" "現在還早，我們八點鐘再去。"

According to the Chinese educational system, an academic year is divided into two semesters. In universities the first semester commences in early September, and the second semester starts in February the following year.

四、看圖會話 Talk About These Pictures

1. Talking about the past experience

學過⋯　來過⋯　　　　　　　看過⋯

2. Describing the continuation of an action or a state

坐著…　拿著…　　　放著…　拿著…

3. Talking about the duration of an action or a state

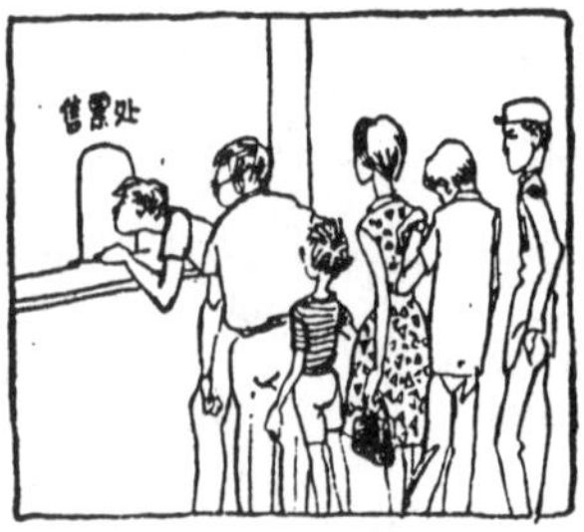

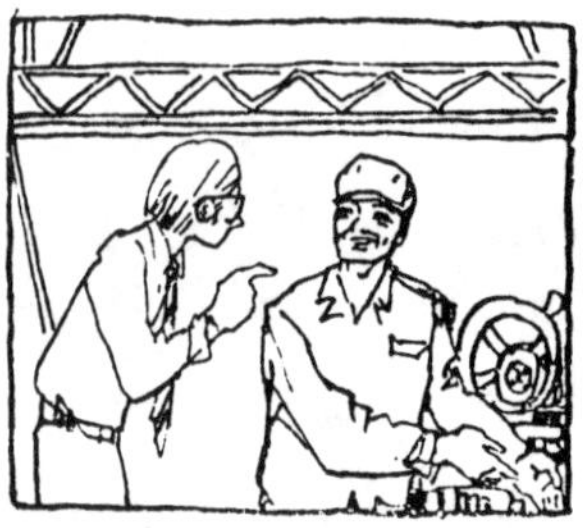

等了……　　　工作了……

來了……　　　住了……

4. Indicating the changed circumstance

綠了……　　　……了

開了……　　　不……了

(107,108)

5. Giving a description of the action

著急地　　　　　　　　　熱情地

五、語法小結　**A Brief Summary of Grammar**

1. The aspects of verbs

Chinese verbs are not conjugated. The time of an action (past, present or future) is shown by time words. The various aspects of an action (impending, progressive, continuous, conclusive or showing past experience) are expressed by aspect particles, adverbs, optative verbs or modal particles. So far five types of verbal aspects have been dealt with.

(1) " 要…了 ", " 快要…了 " or " 就要…了 " are generally used to indicate an impending action, e.g.

飛機就要起飛了。

快要放寒假了。

二月十二號就要考試了。

他的理想要實現了。

" 正在 ", " 正 ", " 在 " or " 正在…呢 " are used to represent an action as in progress, e.g.
as in progress, e.g.

我正在看電視呢。

現在梅花正開著呢。

我去的時候，有人在打電話呢。

我唸那首詩呢。

(3) The continuation of an action or a state is expressed by "著". Its negative form is "沒有…著", e.g.

郵局的門還開著呢。

下午咖啡館裏坐著很多人。

孩子們唱著歌兒回家。

行李上沒有寫著他的名字。

(4) "了" denotes a concluded action. Its negative form is "沒有…", e.g.

電影開始了嗎?

你們開學了嗎?

今天的報我已經看了。

那封信你寄了沒有?

(5) Past experience is described by "過". Its negative form is "沒有…過", e.g.

我還沒有去過醫務所呢。

他以前當過營業員。

你學過什麼專業?

我沒有用中文寫過詩。

2. Adverbial modifiers and the structural particle "地"

(1) Adverbs normally do not need a "地" after them in order to function as adverbial modifiers, e.g.

我也得過肺炎。

他們常常利用假期工作。

(2) When used adverbially, monosyllabic adjectives generally do not take a "地" after them; but dissyllabic adjectives do. "地" is always attached to an adjective that functions adverbially but that is itself preceded by an adverbial modifier. E.g.

學習外語要多說、多聽。

代表們認真地了解了這個大學的情況。

他希望以後能更好地研究中國文化。

(3) A noun indicating time, when used adverbially, does not have a "地" attached to it, e.g.

老師晚上輔導我們。

你們幾號放假?

(4) A prepositional construction used adverbially is not followed by "地", e.g.

我給家裏人寄了很多照片。

讓我們為加深兩國人民的了解作更多的工作。

3. The adverbs "再" and "還"

(1) "再" indicates that an action or an event is going to continue or take place again, e.g.

請再吃點兒吧?

您再坐一會兒吧。

再過兩個星期就要開學了。

請你再唸一遍。

他明天不再去了。

(2) "再" indicates also that an action will occur after a certain point or period of time, e.g.

他們先在這兒學習一學期，以後再到北京大學學習專業。

你吃了飯再走吧。

Note that the above examples show two uses of "再", all of which indicate actions that have not yet taken place.

(1) "還" may be used to mean "besides", "in addition (to)" and the like.

閱覽室有中文雜誌、中文報，還有七本漢語詞典。

假期裏我想復習復習語法，還要看幾本中文書。

(2) "還" also signifies the continuation of an action or a state, e.g.

還早呢，我們等一會兒再走。

快十二點了，他還沒有睡呢。

(3) "還" may also be used to indicate that an action (mostly in interrogative sentences or sentences with optative verbs) will be repeated, e.g.

這個電影你還想看第三遍嗎？

明天你還去頤和園嗎？

六、練習　Exercises

1. Fill in the following blanks with a proper word to form words or phrases:

天：＿＿天，＿＿天，＿＿天，＿＿天，＿＿天，＿＿天，＿＿天，＿＿天

學：學＿＿，＿＿學＿＿，＿＿學，＿＿學，＿＿學，學＿＿，學＿＿＿

文：＿＿文，＿＿文，＿＿文，＿＿文，文＿＿，文＿＿＿

假：＿＿假，＿＿假，＿＿假，假＿＿＿

語：＿＿語，＿＿語，＿＿語，＿＿語，＿＿語，語＿＿，＿＿語，語＿＿＿

飯：＿＿飯，＿＿飯，＿＿飯，＿＿飯

2. Expand the following sentences by adding to them expressions from the list, using the particle "地" whenever you think it is needed:

認真　高興　更多　熱情　大聲　著急

(1) 服務員問我們要什麼。

(2) 大夫檢查他的心臟。

(3) 帕蘭卡問古波："媽媽的信呢？快給我！"

(4) 他告訴我，這次他的考試成績很好。

(5) 王老師讓他唸課文。

(6) 最近她身體不太好，要參加鍛鍊。

3. Fill in the following blanks with a word from the brackets:

(1) 昨天我吃了飯＿＿去醫務所了。（再　就）

(2) 我們＿＿上一個月的課就放暑假了。（還　再）

(3) 外邊＿下雪嗎？（還　再）

(4) 時間還早，你休息一下兒＿去吧。（再　就）

(5) 這張明信片很好，我＿想買一些。（再　還）

(6) 這些練習很難，我想＿檢查一遍。（又　再）

(7) 已經十二點了，誰＿在唱歌？（再　還）

(8) 這個詞我＿忘了。（再　又）

(9) 明天＿颱風嗎？（還　再）

(10) 他＿要在這兒學習兩年。（再　還）

4. Translate the following sentences into Chinese:

(1) He is wearing a pair of new shoes today.

(2) This clerk used to work in that post office.

(3) After studying this poem you will know something about the writer.

(4) The doctor is attending him right now.

(5) The plum trees will soon begin to blossom.

(6) Who is knocking at the door?

(7) The wind is blowing, and it will soon rain.

(8) Did you take any of the pictures here?

(9) He earned some money by working during the vacation.

(10) Don't stand there like that, sit down please.

5. Fill in the following blanks with the particles "了", "著" or "過":

有兩個小孩兒在樹下邊坐＿唸英語。一個穿＿白襯衫，

一個穿＿綠襯衫。我站＿聽他們唸，他們唸得很慢、很清楚。

穿白襯衫的孩子不唸＿，他大聲地説：「你唸得不對。」

穿綠襯衫的孩子也著急地説：「你錯＿，我沒錯。書上寫＿

呢，這個詞我們學＿。」這時候，我笑＿問這個孩子：「這

個詞你學＿嗎？你再看一看書吧。"他拿＿＿書，認真地看了看，說："我錯＿＿。"

　　我問他們："你們學＿＿多長時間的英語＿＿？"他們說："我們學＿＿兩年＿＿。"我說："你們很努力，一定能學得很好。"

6. Correct the following sentences:

    (1) 他很長時間病了。

    (2) 這個問題應該回答這樣。

    (3) 小張在河邊釣魚著。

    (4) 我看兩次了那個電影。

    (5) 她站著在前邊。

    (6) 他以前到過英國學英文。

    (7) 我以前不會照相了，現在會照相。

    (8) 古波要學習中文很努力。

7. Describe briefly what you did during the last summer (winter) vacation.

七、語音語調 Pronunciation and Intonation

1. Rhythm

Rhythm is determined by the alternation of long and short vowels, strong and weak elements or of stressed and unstressed syllables in speech flow. In Chinese the rhythm of multi-syllabic words is fairly marked and regular. Generally multi-syllabic words have about the same length. A multi-syllabic word containing more characters is uttered rapidly and one with fewer characters is uttered slowly. The length of weak stressed syllables is short and that of stressed ones is long. Here is a number of rules about length and rhythm:

(1) In dissyllabic words the length of the stressed syllable is twice as long as that of the unstressed one. Assuming the time needed for uttering a certain word is 6, and the word is pronounced in the medium-strong pattern, then the distribution of time should be 2:4, e.g.

生命　機會　天氣　時間　著急　學校

寒假　詩歌　華僑　考試　暑假　檢查

實現　國際　利用　奇怪

In the strong-weak pattern, the distribution of time would be 4:2, e.g.

眼睛　耳朵　鼻子　知識　朋友　學生

先生　孩子

(2) In a trisyllabic word, when the first two syllables are uttered in quick succession, this trisyllabic word may be said to be structured on a "2+1" pattern, in which case, the last syllable takes about the same length of time as the preceding two syllables. If the trisyllabic word is to be pronounced in the medium-weak-strong pattern, the distribution of time should be 2:1:3, e.g.

醫務所　收音機　圖書館　頤和園

天安門　外語系

(3) Most quadrisyllabic words follow the "2+2" pattern. The stressed syllable takes up half of the total length of time needed for all four syllables. If the quadrisyllable is to be uttered in the medium-weak-medium-strong pattern, the distribution of time should be 1.5:0.5:1:3. E.g.

北京大學　語言學院　社會主義

(120,121)

2. Sense group stress (6)

(1) In a Subject + Verb + Complement construction, the complement is stressed. E.g.

我工作了三個小時。

他教書教了三十多年。

去年我透視過一次。

(2) In subjectless sentences, the object is stressed. E.g.

要颶風了。

現在下雨了。　　　　(When the adverbial adjunct is at the beginning of a sentence, it is not stressed.)

有人敲門。　　　　　(The pivotal word is not stressed.)

(3) In a Subject + Verb + Object construction where the object consists of several coordinate elements, all the coordinate elements are stressed. E.g.

他們到過長城和北海。

還要檢查一下兒眼睛、耳朵。

3. Read aloud the following poem:

我們歡唱 (huānchàng to sing merrily)，我們翱翔 (áoxiáng to soar)。

我們翱翔，我們歡唱。

一切 (yíqiè all) 的一切，常在歡唱。

一的一切，常在歡唱。

是你在歡唱? 是我在歡唱?

是他在歡唱? 是火 (huǒ fire) 在歡唱?

歡唱在歡唱!

歡唱在歡唱!

只有 (zhǐyǒu only) 歡唱!

只有歡唱!

歡唱!

　歡唱!

　　歡唱!

（節選自郭沫若《鳳凰涅槃》）

第三十六課

一、課　文

這套茶具比那套便宜

帕蘭卡：古波，我們去百貨大樓，好嗎？我要買茶具。

古　波：學校旁邊有個商店，為什麼去百貨大樓呢？

帕蘭卡：這個商店我去過了，東西不太多。百貨大樓比這個商店大，東西也比這兒多。

古　波：好吧，我也想去買自行車。

（在百貨大樓）

帕蘭卡：同志，我要一套瓷器茶具。

售貨員：好，您看看這套，這是江西景德鎮的。

古　波：景德鎮的瓷器非常有名。

售貨員：對了。景德鎮生產瓷器的歷史很長了，質量非常好。有人說那兒的瓷器比玉白，比紙薄。

帕蘭卡：是啊，作得真漂亮！這種茶具一套多少錢？

售貨員：這套六個茶碗，一共四十二塊二毛八（分）。

帕蘭卡：有比這個便宜的嗎？

售貨員：這套唐山的茶具比那套便宜。

古　　波：質量有那套好嗎？

售貨員：質量也不錯。茶壺沒那個大，只有四個茶碗。唐山瓷器生產的歷史沒有景德鎮長，可是解放以後有了很大的發展，質量比以前提高了。

帕蘭卡：我覺得茶壺上的畫兒比那套畫得好。

售貨員：這是齊白石的畫兒。茶壺茶碗都好看，也很便宜，一共三十塊零四毛。

帕蘭卡：好，我要這套。

售貨員：您這是三十二塊，找您一塊六（毛）。

古　　波：請問，買自行車在哪兒？

售貨員：在外邊，大樓旁邊。

帕蘭卡：謝謝您。

售貨員：不謝。

二、生　詞

1. 套　　　　tào　　　　a measure word, set

2. 茶具　　　chájù　　　tea set; tea service

3. 便宜　　　piányi　　　cheap

4. 自行車　　zìxíngchē　　bicycle; bike

5.瓷器	cíqì	chinaware; porcelain
6.售貨員	shòuhuòyuán	shop assistant
貨	huò	goods; commodity
7.生產	shēngchǎn	to produce; to manufacture
8.歷史	lìshǐ	history
9.質量	zhíliàng	quality
10.玉	yù	jade
11.薄	báo	thin
12.種	zhǒng	a measure word, kind; type; sort
13.茶碗	cháwǎn	teacup
碗	wǎn	bowl; a measure word, bowl
14.一共	yígòng	altogether; in all
15.塊（元）	kuài (yuán)	a measure word (a Chinese monetary unit, equal to 10 jiǎo or máo)
16.毛（角）	máo (jiǎo)	a measure word (a Chinese monetary unit, equal to 10 fēn)
17.分	fēn	a measure word (the smallest Chinese monetary unit)
18.茶壺	cháhú	teapot
壺	hú	pot; a measure word
19.只	zhǐ	only

20.解放	jiěfàng	to liberate, liberation
21.發展	fāzhǎn	to develop
22.提高	tígāo	to increase; to improve
23.畫兒	huàr	picture; painting
24.畫	huà	to paint
25.零	líng	zero
26.找（錢）	zhǎo (qián)	to give change

專　名

1.百貨大樓	Bǎihuò Dàlóu	The (Beijing) Department Store
2.江西	Jiāngxī	name of a Chinese province
3.景德鎮	Jǐngdézhèn	name of a Chinese city
4.唐山	Tángshān	name of a Chinese city
5.齊白石	Qí Báishí	name of a person

補　充　詞

1.貴	guì	expensive
2.厚	hòu	thick
3.訂	dìng	to subscribe to (a newspaper, etc.)
4.零錢	língqián	change (said of money)
5.價錢	jiàqián	price

6. 畫蛇添足	huàshétiānzú	(fig.) ruin the effect by adding what is superfluous
7. 別人	biéren	other people; others
8. 腳	jiǎo	foot

三、閱讀短文

畫 蛇 添 足*

　　古時候，有幾個朋友在一起喝酒。他們人很多，可是酒太少，只有一壺。這壺酒給誰喝呢？有人說：" 我們每人都畫一條蛇(shé snake)，大家比一比，看誰畫得快。畫得最快的人喝這壺酒，好嗎？"

　　大家都說：" 好。"

　　他們開始畫蛇了。有一個年輕人比別人*畫得快，他看別人*還在畫呢，就指著自己畫的蛇高興地說：" 你們畫得太慢了！看，我現在還有時間，讓我再給蛇添(tiān to add)幾隻(zhī a measure word) 腳吧。"

　　這時候，旁邊的一個人大聲地說：" 我已經畫完(huà wán finish) 了，這壺酒應該給我喝。"

　　年輕人一聽，著急地說：" 你畫得沒有我快，我早就畫完了。你看，我還給蛇添了幾隻腳*呢。這壺酒該我喝。"

　　那個人笑著說：" 人人都知道蛇沒有腳*。你現在畫了腳*，就不是蛇了，所以第一個畫完蛇的是我。"

　　大家都說："他說得對，這壺酒應該給他。"

　　一個人作了多餘 (duōyú superfluous; uncalled for) 的事兒，就叫"畫蛇添足(zú foot)"。

四、注釋 Notes

1. "這種茶具一套多少錢?"

"How much is a tea set of this kind?"

This is one way to ask the prices of goods. Another way is "這種茶具多少錢一套?" And the reply is usually "一套四十二塊二毛八" (or "四十二塊二毛八一套").

2. "一共四十二塊二毛八 (分) 。"

The counting units of Renminbi are "元" (yúan), "角" (jiǎo) and "分" (fēn), or "塊" (kuài), "毛" (máo) and "分" (fēn) in spoken Chinese. One kuai is equal to ten mao, and one mao to ten fen. Máo (jiǎo) or fen, when at the end of a figure, is usually left out in colloquial speech, e.g.

5.20 元—五塊二 (毛)

26.37 元—二十六塊三毛七 (分)

A single-unit figure often ends in colloquial speech, with an additional word "錢", e.g. "十五塊錢", "兩毛錢", "八分錢".

If "2 毛" appears between two units in a figure, "2" is pronounced as "二". However, if it appears right at the beginning of a figure, it should be read as "兩". "2分" is pronounced as "二分" when it appears at the end of a figure, but when it stands alone, both "二分" and "兩分" are correct. E.g. "兩塊二毛二", "兩毛二分", "二分錢", "兩分錢".

3. "解放以後有了很大的發展。"

"It has developed greatly since liberation."

"解放以後" is generally understood to mean "since the founding of the new China."

4. "這是齊白石的畫兒。"

Qi Baishi (1863 – 1957), a well-known Chinese painter, was born to a poor peasant family in Xiangtan, Hunan Province. Young Qi could afford only a six-month education. At the age of twelve, he began working as a flower carver. He had a very good mastery of traditional Chinese painting, and was so full of creative spirit that he developed a style of his own. After liberation the People's Government conferred on him the title of "the outstanding artist of the Chinese people".

5.　"一共三十塊零四毛。"

When "塊" is preceded by integer above ten, or when "塊" is absent between "塊" and "分", "零" should be placed after "塊", and the last unit is never omitted, e.g.

> 10.50 元—十塊零五毛
>
> 40.07 元—四十塊零七分
>
> 3.02 元—三塊零二分

6.　"您這是三十二塊，找您一塊六（毛）。"

"You've given me 32 yuan, and I'll give you 1.6 yuan change."

五、替換與擴展　Substitution and Extension

(一)

1. 這種自行車怎麼樣？

　這種自行車比那種便宜。

茶壺（種），	小
明信片（套），	新
玉（種），	貴*
詩（首），	容易
售貨員（位），	熱情
作家（位），	年輕

(133,134)　　　　　　　　　— 88 —

2. 今天比昨天冷嗎？
　　今天不比昨天冷。

你，	他，	大
北海，	頤和園，	遠
漢語，	法語，	難
今年暑假，	去年，	長
這套郵票，	那套，	舊
這本詞典，	那本，	薄

3. 瓷器的質量比以前提高了沒有？
　　瓷器的質量比以前提高了。

工廠的生產，	發展
兩國人民的了解，	加深
考試的成績，	提高
天氣，	熱
這學期，	忙
他的信，	多

4. 你唱歌兒唱得很好，是嗎？
　　哪裡，他唱歌兒唱得比我好。

考試，	好
滑冰，	快
畫畫兒，	好
看歷史書，	多

5. 這個茶碗有那個大嗎?
   這個茶碗沒有那個大。

錶（種），	好看
梅花（束），	漂亮
白襯衫（件），	長
自行車（種），	好
學校（個），	大
漢語書（本），	厚*

6. 這種茶具一套多少錢?
   三十塊零四毛。

信封（個），	0.02	元
圖片（套），	2.08	元
裙子（條），	20.70	元
鞋（雙）	18.00	元
啤酒（瓶），	0.74	元
麵包（個），	0.15	元

(二)

1. Subscribing to a magazine

   A：請問，訂*雜誌在哪兒?

   B：你到對面的郵局，那兒可以訂*報、訂*雜誌。

   A：謝謝您。

   *   *   *

   A：同志，現在可以訂*《人民文學》雜誌嗎?

C：可以，你想訂＊多長時間？

A：一年。一共多少錢？

C：一共四塊八。

2. Going shopping

    A：同志，這套明信片多少錢？

    B：八毛三。

    A：我要兩套。

    B：您還要什麼？

    A：要十張八分的郵票。

    B：一共兩塊四毛六。

    A：我沒有零錢＊，請您找吧。

    B：好，找您七塊五毛四。

                    ＊   ＊   ＊

    A：您要什麼？

    B：請問，有中國紅葡萄酒嗎？

    A：沒有了。您看，這種葡萄酒也很好，質量不比中國
        紅葡萄酒差（chà bad; poor），價錢＊比那種便宜。

    B：多少錢一瓶？

    A：兩塊八。

    B：是北京的嗎？

    A：不，是上海的。

    B：好，我先買一瓶嘗嘗。

3. Talking about the weather

    A：你們國家夏天天氣怎麼樣？

B：夏天時間比這兒長，天氣也比這兒熱。你們那兒有
　　沒有這兒熱?

A：沒有這兒熱，熱的時間也沒有這兒長。天氣最熱的
　　時候，大家都離開城裏了，那時候農村比城裏人多。

*　　　*　　　*

六、語法　Grammar

1.　"比" used to express comparison (1)

The preposition "比" may be used to express comparison between two objects.　The following table shows the position of "比" in sentences with an adjectival predicate.

Noun or pronoun (1)	Preposition "比"	Noun or pronoun (2)	Adjective
他	比	我	忙。
這個房間	比	那個房間	大。
今天的課文	比	昨天的課文	難。

"比" may also be used to express comparison in some sentences with a verbal predicate:

Noun or pronoun (1)	Preposition "比"	Noun or pronoun (2)	Verb	Noun or pronoun
古波 我朋友 他們班	比 比 比	帕蘭卡 我 你們班	注意 了解 喜歡踢	語法。 中國的情況。 足球。

If the verb has a complement of degree, "比…" may be used before either the verb or the complement, e.g.

他比我走得快。

（他走得比我快。）

大學生隊比銀行隊踢得好。

（大學生隊踢得比銀行隊好。）

If the verb has both an object and a complement of degree, "比" may be used before either the repeated verb, or the complement, e.g.

他們班準備考試比我們班準備得早。

（他們班準備考試準備得比我們班早。）

他作菜比他愛人作得好。

（他作菜作得比他愛人好。）

— 93 —

(141,142)

The adverb "不" is put before "比" to form a negative comparative sentence:

這件襯衫不比那件新。

我每天不比他來得早。

Note that in an adjective-predicate sentence containing "比…", adverbs like "很", "真" or "非常" are never used before the predicate adjective (it is wrong, for example, to say "他比我很忙"). But adverbs of degree such as "更" or "還" may be used (we may say, for example, "他比我更忙").

2. "有" or "沒有" used to express comparison

The verbs "有" and "沒有" can also be used to express comparison:

Noun or pronoun (1)	The verb "有" or "沒有"	Noun or pronoun (2)	Adjective	Other elements
你的孩子 這兒 這個地方	有 沒有 沒有	他的孩子 北京 頤和園	大 冷。 有意思。	嗎?

This type of comparison, often used in negative or interrogative sentences, indicates the extent to which two things are similar or dissimilar.

Points to be noted:

(1) In addition to sentences with an adjectival predicate, "有…" can also be used in some sentences with a verbal predicate to express comparison. In these sentences "有…" has the same position as "比", e.g.

她沒有我喜歡古典音樂。

你跳舞跳得沒有他好。

我起床沒有他起得早。

(2) "沒有…" and "不比…" are different in meaning, for example, "他沒有我來得早" means "He did not come as early as I did". But "他不比我來得早" means either "He came later than I did" or "He came at the same time as I did".

七、練習 Exercises

1. Read aloud the following phrases:

發展生產　　發展文化　　努力發展

發展得很快　有了很大發展

提高生產　　提高質量　　努力提高

提高得很快　有了很大提高

生產瓷器　　生產自行車　工廠的生產

現代化生產　生產的情況

中國歷史　京劇的歷史　頤和園的歷史

研究歷史　了解歷史

比這兒遠　比這套舊　　比這件小

比他著急　比小張喜歡　比昨天冷

比以前提高　比去年發展　比現在忙

2. Rewrite the following sentences with "比":

(1) 這種筆便宜，那種筆不便宜。

(2) 他的歷史知識多，我的歷史知識少。

(3) 這學期他進步得快，我進步得慢。

(4) 我每天十點睡覺，我哥哥十一點睡覺。

(5) 今年他二十三歲，他朋友二十歲。

(6) 古波看過十次中國電影，帕蘭卡只看過五次。

(7) 昨天很熱，今天更熱。

(8) 他會開車，他妹妹更會開車。

3. Rewrite the following sentences turning them into comparison sentences expressed by "沒有":

(1) 這種自行車的質量比那種好。

(2) 我今年比去年更忙。

(3) 這個郵局大，我們學校的郵局小。

(4) 他的成績比我好。

(5) 那個女同志寫字比這個男同志寫得好看。

(6) 我同學比我身體健康。

4. Describing the pictures:

(1)  比

(2)  不比

(3)

沒
有

(4) 有……嗎?

5. Making conversation in groups:

Example　詞典　4.50元　兩本　10.00元

　　　→A：這種詞典一本多少錢?

　　　　B：四塊五。

　　　　A：我要兩本。

　　　　B：一共九塊。您這是十塊，找您一塊。

(1) 礦泉水 0.57 元　　　5瓶　　　　5.00 元
(2) 帽子　6.05 元　　　1頂　　　　10.00 元
(3) 襯衫　15.80 元　　　3件　　　　50.00 元
(4) 郵票　4.10 元　　　兩套　　　　9.00 元
(5) 地圖　1.52 元　　　10張　　　　20.00 元

6. Give the main facts in the following dialogue in a short account:

A：這兩個自行車工廠哪個大?

B：這個廠的歷史沒有那個長，那是一個老廠，這是一個新
廠。新廠比老廠大，工人也比老廠多。

A：新廠的年輕工人比老工人多吧？

B：是啊！年輕工人比老工人多。這個廠一共有五百多工人，年輕的就有三百多。

A：新廠的生產情況怎麼樣？

B：新廠的生產今年比去年有了很大的發展，質量比以前有了很大的提高。

第三十七課

一、課　文

這件跟那件一樣長

古　波：同志，我看看布中山裝。

售貨員：您穿的嗎？給您這件，請到對面試試。

古　波：太短了。

售貨員：這件比那件大五公分，您再試試。

古　波：長短很合適，可是比那件肥得多。

售貨員：我給您找一件瘦一點兒的。您看這件，跟那件一樣長，比那件瘦三公分。

帕蘭卡：這件很合適。你穿了中山裝就跟中國人一樣了。

古　波：不，鼻子、眼睛還跟中國人不一樣。你看衣服的顏色怎麼樣？

帕蘭卡：藍的沒有灰的好看。有灰的嗎？

售貨員：有。

古　波：好，我要灰的。多少錢一件？

－ 99 －

(153,154)

售貨員：九塊九毛五。請您到那個窗口交錢。

帕蘭卡：同志，有我穿的中式小棉襖嗎？

售貨員：有。您要什麼面兒的？

帕蘭卡：我要綢面兒的，上次我在這兒看過。

售貨員：綢面兒的現在沒有，您一個星期以後再來看看。要不，您定作吧，十天就可以了。

古　波：買衣服也要下星期來，定作比買只多三天，還是定作吧。

售貨員：作的比買的還要合適一些。您先到三層去看看綢子，那兒有很多種。

帕蘭卡：您看我要買幾米綢子？

售貨員：您比我高一點兒，買兩米半吧。

帕蘭卡：好，謝謝您。

　　　　　　＊　　　　　＊　　　　　＊

帕蘭卡：啊，五點三刻了。

古　波：你的錶快五分鐘。

帕蘭卡：不早了，快回學校吧。今天花了不少錢，一共花了一百零五塊。

古　波：我還買了一輛自行車呢，比你多花七十多塊。好，我現在就騎車回學校。

帕蘭卡：你認識路嗎？騎車要注意點兒。

古　波：你放心吧。

二、生　詞

1.一樣	yíyàng	same; identical
2.布	bù	cotton cloth
3.中山裝	zhōngshān～zhuāng	Chinese tunic suit
4.短	duǎn	short
5.公分	gōngfēn	a measure word, centimeter
6.長短	chángduǎn	length
7.合適	héshì	suitable; fit
8.肥	féi	loose-fitting; fat
9.瘦	shòu	tight; thin; lean
10.衣服	yīfu	clothes; clothing
11.顏色	yánsè	colour
12.藍	lán	blue
13.灰	huī	grey
14.交	jiāo	to pay (money)
15.中式	zhōngshì	Chinese style
16.棉襖	mián'ǎo	cotton-padded jacket
17.面兒	miànr	cover; outside
18.綢（子）	chóu(zi)	silk fabric

19.上（次）	shàng (cì)	last (time); a previous (occasion)
20.要不	yàobù	or; or else; otherwise
21.定作	dìngzuò	to have something made to order
22.下（星期）	xià (xīngqī)	next (week)
23.米	mǐ	a measure word, meter
24.高	gāo	tall
25.花	huā	to spend (money)
26.輛	liàng	a measure word for vehicles
27.騎	qí	to ride (a bicycle)

補　充　詞

1.毛衣	máoyī	woollen sweater
2.雨衣	yǔyī	raincoat
3.西裝	xīzhuāng	Western-style suit
4.料子	liàozi	material
5.襪子	wàzi	socks; stockings
6.旗袍	qípáo	Chinese-style frock
7.胖	pàng	fat; stout; plump
8.布鞋	bùxié	cloth shoes

三、閱讀短文

"高一點兒" (相聲)

A：這不是老張嗎？

B：是我啊，您好！

A：你好。聽説(tīngshuō to hear) 你也開始寫相聲(xiàngsheng comic dialogue) 了？

B：我寫得很少，去年只寫了三個很短的相聲，您呢？

A：我工作很忙，也寫得不多。去年只寫了十三個不太短的相聲。

B：您比我多寫了十個！我要向(xiàng from) 您學習。

A：不客氣。你寫相聲有問題，就來找我吧。你最近翻譯了一本書，是嗎？

B：我翻譯了一本很薄的書，只有一百多頁 (yè page)。

A：我也翻譯了一本很薄的書。

B：多少頁？

A：只有四百多頁。

B：比我的多三百多頁，我要向您學習。

A：不客氣，以後你翻譯有問題，就來找我吧。你穿的棉襖是什麼面兒的？

B：是布的。

A：我穿的是綢面兒的。

B：你的比我的好。

Ａ：不客氣。你今年多大？

Ｂ：我今年二十八，您呢？

Ａ：我今年二十九。

Ｂ：比我大一歲。

Ａ：不客氣。你多高？

Ｂ：我一米七〇，您呢？

Ａ：我現在一米七一，比你高一點兒。

Ｂ：是啊，您總是比我高一點兒。

Ａ：不客氣，你的錶現在幾點？

Ｂ：九點半。

Ａ：我的錶現在十點半。

Ｂ：你的錶也比我們大家的錶快一個小時！

Ａ：不客氣。——啊？

四、注釋　Notes

1. "您穿的嗎？"

   "For yourself?"

2. "長短很合適。"

   "It's just the right length."

Here "長短" refers to "length". In Chinese a monosyllabic adjective may often combine with an antonym to form a noun indicating certain characteristics of things referred to. The noun "大小", "肥瘦" and "快慢" are words so formed.

3. "可是比那件肥得多。"

The adjective "肥" means "loose" (of clothes) or "fat" (of animals or meat). To describe a stout person, the word "胖" is used instead of "肥", which is derogatory. "瘦" (thin) however, may be used for both people and animals.

4. "上次我在這兒看過。"

The noun "上" (meaning "previous") or "下" (meaning "next") can be used to indicate the order of time, or sequence of events, such as in "上次", "下次", "上月", "下月", "上星期五", "下星期五", etc.

5. "要不，您定作吧。"

In spoken Chinese the conjunction "要不" is used to indicate a choice between two things, two contrary possibilities or two entirely different results. For instance, one may say "你明天八點一定到，要不，我們就出發了。"

6. "定作比買只多三天，還是定作吧。"

   "It'll only take three days more to have your jacket made to measure. It would be wise of you to do so."

Here "還是" expresses the speaker's wish, implying that it would be better to do something in the way he suggests. Hence we may say "今天太冷，你還是多穿點兒衣服吧。"

— 105 —   (158,159,160)

7. "您看我要買幾米綢子?"

"How many metres of silk do you think I should buy?"

Sometimes the verb "看" may be used to express an opinion on the basis of observation, e.g. "你看這樣好不好?" "我看可以。"

8. "今天花了不少錢,一共花了一百零五塊。"

The naming of numerals above one hundred is as follows:

```
九十…………九十七………一百
一百零一……一百零五……一百一十
一百一十一…一百八十…三百六十…
六百七十一…七百四十五…八百九十九
九百…………九百五十三…九百九十九
```

五、替換與擴展 Substitution and Extension

㈠

1. 你的棉襖跟他的棉襖一樣不一樣?

我的棉襖跟他的不一樣。

```
筆    衣服
錶    專業
病    地址
```

2 <u>這件衣服</u>比<u>那件</u><u>長</u>嗎？

這件跟那件一樣長。

你，	她，	大
他，	你，	高
你們國家，	這兒，	熱
你們班的學生，	他們班，	多
從這兒到學校，	從那兒，	遠
你學漢語的時間，	他，	長
這種布的顏色，	那種，	漂亮

3. 這輛自行車跟那輛一樣<u>新</u>嗎？

不，這輛比那輛<u>舊一點兒</u>。

飛機（種），	快，	慢得多
問題（個），	難，	容易點兒
樹（種），	多，	少得多
茶具 （套），	便宜，	便宜點兒
綢子 （種），	薄，	薄得多
毛衣*（件），	大，	小得多

4. 這件中山裝比那件長多少?

　　這件中山裝比那件長<u>五公分</u>。

棉襖（件），	肥，	三公分
裙子（條），	瘦，	兩公分
帽子（頂），	小，	半公分
襯衫（件），	大，	一號
雨衣（件），	短，	一點兒

穿，	少穿，	一件衣服
寫，	多寫，	一張紙
學，	少學，	一種外語
吃，	多吃，	一個麵包

5. 你跟他<u>花</u>得一樣多嗎?

　　我比他<u>多花</u><u>七十多塊</u>。

6. 這種<u>綢子</u>多少錢<u>一米</u>?

　　這種綢子<u>三塊八</u>一米。

自行車（輛），	174 元
布（米），	2.85 元
瓷器（套），	208 元
西裝＊（套），	135 元
料子＊（米），	38.76 元
襪子＊（雙），	3.20 元

（二）

1. At the tailor's

    A：同志，我要作一件旗袍*。

    B：好。我給您量一量。

    A：不，這件旗袍是給我姐姐的。她沒有來過中國。我
    要送她一件中式衣服，您看能作嗎?

    B：您知道她穿多大的衣服?

    A：她跟我一樣高，比我胖一點兒。我的衣服她也能穿。

    B：好吧，我們試一試。

    A：太感謝您了。

2. Buying shoes

    A：同志，讓我看看那種布鞋*。

    B：您穿多大號的?

    A：我穿 27 公分的。我不知道是多大號的。

    B：您試試這雙，四十一號半，合適嗎?

    A：小了點兒。

    B：您再試試這雙，四十二號的。

    A：這雙真合適。多少錢一雙?

    B：四塊五毛五。

3. Running into somebody one hasn't seen for a long time

    A：很長時間沒見了，你比以前胖*一點兒了。

    B：你身體好嗎? 你還跟以前一樣年輕。

    A：哪裏，我比你老得多。

4. Exchanging amenities

A：你來了一年多了吧？在這兒覺得怎麼樣？

B：很好。這兒的人都很熱情，我過得很好，跟在我們
國家一樣。

A：這兒的天氣你覺得怎麼樣？

B：夏天和秋天天氣跟我們那兒一樣，冬天比我們那兒冷
一些。這兒的春天 (chūntiān spring) 風太大，我不太喜
歡。

A：這兒的春天沒有你們那兒暖和 (nuǎnhuo warm)， 也比
你們那兒短，是嗎？
......

C：快十二點了，您在這兒吃飯吧。

B：不用了，我還是早點兒回學校。

A：別客氣，在這兒就跟在自己家裏一樣。請吧。

*　　　*　　　*

廣告
(guǎnggào advertisement)

六、語法　Grammar

1. "跟…一樣" used to express comparison

"跟…一樣" can be used to compare two things that are either identical or similar. The preposition "跟" introduces the second part of a comparison. The adjective "一樣" functions as the main part of the predicate. The whole structure "跟…一樣" may also serve as an adverbial modifier.

Noun or pronoun (1)	"跟"	Noun or pronoun (2)	"一樣"	Adjective
這本詞典	跟	那本（詞典）	一樣。	
他	跟	我	一樣	忙。
這兒的梅花	跟	那兒（的梅花）	一樣	多。

If the two nouns in a comparison both have modifiers before them, the second noun (sometimes even the structural particle "的") may be omitted.

The affirmative-negative form of the pattern "跟…一樣" is "跟…一樣不一樣". E.g.

這個字跟那個字一樣不一樣?

你跟他一樣不一樣大?

The negative form of the pattern "跟…一樣" is "跟…不一樣" or "不跟…一樣", e.g.

今年冬天的天氣跟去年不一樣。

這個信封跟那個信封不一樣大。

弟弟的專業不跟我一樣。

Note that the expression "跟…一樣" may also function either as an adjective modifier or a complement, e.g.

我要作一件跟你那件一樣的棉襖。

他説漢語説得跟中國人一樣。

2. The complements of quantity

In an adjective-predicate sentence of comparison with "比", the specific differences between two things or people can be expressed by placing after the predicate a numeral-measure word phrase as a complement.

Noun or pronoun (1)	"比"	Noun or pronoun (2)	Adjective	Numeral-measure word phrase
他	比	我	小	三歲。
這種筆	比	那種	便宜	兩塊錢。
這個班	比	那個班	多	五個學生。

The word "一點兒" (or "一些") is used to indicate that the difference between two things or people is very slight. The structural particle "得" together with the complement "多" indicates that the difference is great, e.g.

他今天比昨天好一點兒。

這種布比那種布好看一些。

他弟弟比他年輕得多。

我們這次參觀的地方比上次多得多。

今天的風比昨天小得多了。

In a verb-predicate sentence of comparison, to indicate the difference in concrete terms, adjectives like "早、晚", or "多、少" are used as adverbial modifiers before the verb, and words naming the difference are placed after the verb. E.g.

我只比你早來了五分鐘。

你先走吧，我要晚走一刻鐘。

這個月我們工廠多生產一百五十輛自行車。

他少買了一張電影票，我不去了。

七、練習 Exercises

1. Read aloud the following phrases:

上月　　上星期　上星期日

上半年　上學期　上半學期

下月　　下星期　下星期日

下半年　下學期　下半學期

上次　上一個　上一課　上一封

下次　下一個　下一課　下一封

肥一點兒　瘦一點兒　長一點兒

短一點兒　高一點兒　小一點兒

便宜一些　薄一些　　冷一些

熱一些　　老一些　　年輕一些

高興得多　辛苦得多　著急得多

合適得多　怕得多　　喜歡得多

(172,173)

2. Rewrite the following sentences after the model:

Example 這件中山裝是灰的，那件也是灰的。

→這件中山裝的顏色跟那件一樣。

(1) 他是售貨員，他愛人也是售貨員。

(2) 我以後學歷史，我朋友也學歷史。

(3) 古波買了一本《現代漢語詞典》，帕蘭卡也買了一本《現代漢語詞典》。

(4) 小王今年二十三歲，小張也是二十三歲。

(5) 他學過兩年多的法語，你也學過兩年多的法語。

(6) 我現在一米七五，我弟弟也是一米七五。

3. Complete the following dialogues:

(1) 新工廠有五百四十五個工人，老工廠有四百八十三個工人。

A：新工廠比 _____ ？

B：新工廠比 _____ 六十二個工人。

(2) 這件棉襖長七十八公分，那件棉襖長七十二公分。

A：那件棉襖比 _____ ？

B：那件棉襖比 _____ 六公分。

(3) 他妹妹今年十五歲，他今年十八歲。

A：他比 _____ ？

B：他比 _____ 三歲。

(4) 這輛自行車一百九十四塊，那輛一百七十四塊。

A：那輛比 _____ ？

B：那輛比 _____ 二十塊。

(173,174,175)

(5) 小張六點一刻到學校，他同學六點二十分到學校。

　　A：小張比 ＿＿＿＿＿＿ ？

　　B：小張比 ＿＿＿＿＿＿ 五分鐘。

(6) 上學期我們班學了二十六課，他們班學了二十八課。

　　A：我們班比 ＿＿＿＿＿＿ ？

　　B：我們班比 ＿＿＿＿＿＿ 兩課。

4. Give negative answers to the following questions:

(1) 你騎車跟他騎得一樣快嗎？

(2) 這種布的質量跟那種布一樣嗎？

(3) 他說中國話說得跟中國人一樣嗎？

(4) 你這個月花的錢跟上個月花的一樣多嗎？

(5) 你們國家首都的天氣跟這兒一樣不一樣？

(6) 他們學校開學的時間跟你們學校一樣嗎？

5. Translate the following sentences into Chinese:

(1) How much is the cloth per metre?（多少）

(2) Your shoes are a bit smaller than mine. They don't fit my feet very nicely.（一點兒）

(3) Clothes that are made to measure in this shop are much nicer than in that shop.（…得多）

(4) It is a bit colder this month than last month.（一些）

(5) It's getting late now. I'll come again next time.（下次）

(6) Can you come here by bike tomorrow? Or shall I take you here in my car?（要不）

6. Ask questions on the following passage and answer them, then describe the pictures giving all the details:

這兩個人我都認識，是我的好朋友。穿藍色中山裝的是

(175,176,177)

大張，穿中式小棉襖的是小王。他們倆跟我一樣，都很喜歡
踢足球。大張比小王大兩歲，他跟小王一樣是外語系法語專
業的學生。他們學習很努力，成績都不錯。小王說法語沒有
大張說得流利，可是語法學得比他好。小王喜歡唱歌、跳舞，
大張跟他不一樣，喜歡看京劇。他們倆想要作的工作也不一
樣，小王想當翻譯，大張想當老師，他覺得教書很有意思。

7. Write a short composition describing two of your friends, showing in
   what way they resemble each other and in what way they differ.

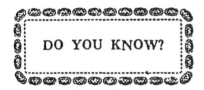
Beijing Cloisonne

China's cloisonne ware is world-renowned for its traditional technique. It flourished in the reign of Jingtai (1450 – 1456) of the Ming Dynasty. The main colour of the enamel used in Jingtai cloisonne is a splended malachite blue from which the term "Jingtai blue" is derived. Cloisonne ware is a product of the traditional metal techniques in combining porcelain and bronze.

Since the founding of the new China the "Jingtai blue" techniques has been much improved and the enamel colour and designs have developed from ten varieties to the present sixty, and various kinds of practical cloisonne wares for practical use have been designed and are now being manufactured.

第三十八課

一、課　文

你　沒　聽　錯　嗎

（在 331 路公共汽車站）

售票員：331 路，開往平安里，請上車。剛上車的同志請買票。

古　波：同志，換 13 路公共汽車在哪兒下車？

售票員：在平安里下車。

古　波：買兩張到平安里的。

售票員：兩毛錢一張票。您這是一塊，找您六毛，請拿好。請大家往裡走，裡邊有座位。下一站，鋼鐵學院，下車的同志請準備好。

古　波：老大爺、大娘，你們請坐。

老大爺：謝謝。

古　波：請問，到平安里還有幾站？

老大爺：這路車的終點站是平安里。你們要去哪兒？

帕蘭卡：我們要去三里屯，到一個中國朋友家。

老大爺：對。下車以後往南走，看見13路汽車站，在那兒等車。你們還要換一次電車。

帕蘭卡：古波，你聽懂了嗎？

古　波：你總不放心，我聽懂了！你看，那兒正修馬路呢。

售票員：前邊要拐彎了，請注意。

老大娘：你們兩位來坐吧，我們下一站下車。

古　波：
帕蘭卡：謝謝！

*　　　　*　　　　*

（在13路汽車站）

古　波：那就是13路汽車站。看，車來了，快跑！

售票員：13路，開往三里河，請排好隊上車。

古　波：啊，三里屯是終點站。

帕蘭卡：你再問問吧。那位老大爺怎麼說要換車呢？你沒聽錯嗎？

古　波：沒有聽錯，快上！同志，買兩張票，到終點站。

*　　　　*　　　　*

售票員：三里河到了，請同志們下車的時候，帶好自己的東西。

帕蘭卡：古波，你看這是三里河，不是三里屯。

古　波：可是咱們坐的是 13 路公共汽車啊！

售票員：你們要去三里屯嗎？方向錯了，你們應該坐往東開的
　　　　車。

帕蘭卡：古波先生，你說你都聽懂了，可是咱們怎麼坐錯了車
　　　　呢。

古　波：別著急，我給你講一個成語故事。

二、生　詞

1.	錯	cuò	wrong
2.	公共汽車	gōnggòng qìchē	bus
	公共	gōnggòng	public
	汽車	qìchē	automobile; car
3.	站	zhàn	(bus) stop
4.	售票員	shòupiàoyuán	ticket seller; conductor
5.	往	wǎng	to go (to a place)
	往	wàng	toward; (train) bound for
6.	剛	gāng	just; only a short while ago
7.	換	huàn	to change
8.	下	xià	to get off (bus, etc.)
9.	座位	zuòwei	seat
10.	大爺	dàye	uncle

11. 大娘	dàniáng	aunt
12. 終點	zhōngdiǎn	terminal point; terminus
13. 南邊	nánbiān	south; southern part
14. 電車	diànchē	trolleybus
15. 修	xiū	to build (road, etc.); to repair
16. 馬路	mǎlù	road; street
馬	mǎ	horse
17. 拐彎	guǎi wān	to turn a corner
18. 跑	pǎo	to run
19. 排隊	pái duì	to line up
20. 怎麼	zěnme	how; why
21. 帶	dài	to take (along); to bring (with)
22. 咱們	zánmen	we
23. 方向	fāngxiàng	direction
24. 東邊	dōngbiān	east; eastern part
25. 講	jiǎng	to tell; to speak; to explain (text, etc.)
26. 故事	gùshi	story

專　名

1. 平安里	Píng'ānlǐ	name of a street in Beijing

2.鋼鐵學院	Gāngtiě Xuéyuàn	The Beijing Iron and steel Engineering Institute
3.三里屯	Sānlǐtún	name of a street in Beijing
4.三里河	Sānlǐhé	name of a street in Beijing

補 充 詞

1.胡同	hútòng	lane; alley
2.紅綠燈	hónglǜdēng	(red and green) traffic light; traffic signal
3.街	jiē	street
4.地鐵	dìtiě	the undergruond; subway
5.西邊	xībian	west; the western part
6.路口	lùkǒu	crossing; intersection
7.北邊	běibian	north; northern part
8.出租汽車	chūzū qìchē	taxi; cab
9.南轅北轍	nányuánběizhé	(fig.) act in a way that defeats one's purpose

三、閱讀課文

南轅北轍[*]

古波問帕蘭卡：" 你知道 ﹒ 南轅 (yuán shafts of a car or a

carriage) 北轍 (zhé rut)’這個成語嗎？”帕蘭卡説：“沒學過。”古波説：“我給你講這個故事吧。”

古時候，有一個人坐著馬車(mǎchē horse-drawn carriage) 到很遠的地方去辦事兒，馬車上放著一個很大的箱子。他讓趕 (gǎn to drive) 車的人不停地趕，馬跑得非常快。

路上，一位老人看見他們，就問：“先生，您這樣著急，要去哪兒？”

“我要去楚國 (Chǔguó Chu State)”，坐車的人大聲地回答。

老人聽了，笑了笑説：“您走錯了。楚國在南邊，您怎麼往北*走呢？”

“沒關係 (méi guānxi that's all right)，”坐車的人説，“您沒看見嗎？我的馬跑得很快。”

“您的馬很好，可是您走的路不對。”

“沒問題，我的馬車是新的，上月剛作好。”

“您的車很新，可是這不是去楚國的路。”

“老大爺，您不知道，”坐車的指著後邊的箱子説，“我的箱子裏放著很多錢。路遠我不怕。”

“您的錢很多，可是別忘了，您走的方向不對。我看，您還是快往回走吧。”

坐車的人一聽，很不高興地説：“我已經走了十天了，您怎麼讓我往回走呢？”他又指著趕車的説：“您看看，他很年輕，身體很好，趕車也趕得非常好，您放心吧。再見！"

　　說著他就讓趕車的趕著車往前走，馬跑得更快了……

　　他們會走到哪兒呢？

　　古波講到這兒，帕蘭卡笑了。她說："他們跟你一樣，也會走到三里河。"

四、注釋　Notes

1. "剛上車的同志請買票。"

   "Fares, please."

Here the adverb "剛" signifies that something happened only a short time ago, e.g. "我剛來一個星期。""他剛走。"

2. "請大家往裏走。"

When pronounced as "wǎng", "往" is a verb, meaning "to go to", as in "我往東（邊），他往西（邊）", "開往城裏" and "飛往北京".

When pronounced as wàng, "往" functions as a preposition, indicating the direction of a movement, as in "往裏走" and "往南走" (in the locative word, "邊" is often omitted).

3. "買兩張到平安里的。"

   "Two (tickets) for Pinganli, please."

4. "老大爺、大娘，你們請坐。"

"大爺 (uncle)" and "大娘 (aunt)" are respectful forms of addresses used for elderly people. "老大爺 (grandpa)" and "老大娘 (granny)" are polite forms of addresses usually for aged strangers.

5. "那位老大爺怎麼說要換車呢？"

   "Why did the grandpa say that we had to change to another bus?"

The interrogative pronoun "怎麼" is often used adverbially to ask about the way something is done (as in "這個詞中文怎麼說"), or the reason why something happens (as in "他怎麼還不來"). In the present text, "怎麼" indicates reason in both cases.

The interrogative pronoun "怎麼樣" is often used as a predicate. It may also function adverbially before a verb, with the same meaning as "怎麼" (as in "這個字怎麼樣寫"), but it is never used in the sense of "why".

6. "三里河到了。"

   "Here you are at Sanlihe."

7. "可是咱們坐的是 13 路公共汽車啊！"

In this sentence "是" is generally uttered with a strong stress to indicate that what is said is true.

The pronoun "咱們" refers to both the speaker and the person spoken to, while a speaker uses "我們" to refer to himself and another or others not including the person spoken to.

五、替換與擴展 Substitution and Extension

㈠

1. <u>那位售票員的話</u>你<u>聽懂</u>了嗎?
　　我聽懂了。

今天的語法課，	聽
這個歌兒，	聽
老師講的故事，	聽
昨天的電影，	看
那本歷史書，	看

2. <u>他家的地址</u>你沒<u>看</u>錯吧?
　　沒有，我沒看錯。

收信人的姓名，	寫
這個練習，	作
老師的問題，	回答
15路電車，	坐
我的帽子，	拿

(190,191,192)

3. 你看見45路汽車站了沒有?

　看見了。就在前邊。

李老師	公共電話
學校的汽車	那條馬路
那兩位留學生	鋼鐵學院

4. 他在說什麼?

　他說："請同志們帶好
　自己的東西。"

拿，	行李
放，	箱子
收，	車票
帶，	孩子

5. 請問電車站在哪兒?

　往南走，很快就到。

左，	拐彎
東，	走
前，	開
東，	拐彎

6. 這個問題很容易，他怎麼沒回答對？

我也不知道。

這首詩，	看懂
今天的課文，	復習好
這個成語，	說對
騎自行車，	學會

（二）

1. Asking the way

A：請問，到花園胡同＊怎麼走？

B：從這兒往前走，前邊有紅綠燈＊，你看見了嗎？到那兒往左拐，在第二條街＊裏。

A：要坐車嗎？

B：不用，走幾分鐘就到了。

A：謝謝你。

　　　＊　　　＊　　　＊

A：請問，地鐵＊車站在哪兒？

B：往西＊走，到路口＊再往北走。

A：離這兒遠嗎？

B：不遠，只有一百多米。

2. Taking a bus

A：車怎麼還不來？已經等了半天 (bàntiān quite a while) 了。

B：別著急。你看，車來了。

     *   *   *

A：同志，買兩張票，到百貨大樓。

C：您坐錯了。這路車不去百貨大樓。您可以在北海公園
　　下車，在那兒換103路電車。

A：謝謝。到站請告訴我們一下兒，好嗎?

C：好，還有三站就到北海公園了。

     *   *   *

A：同志，您下車嗎?

D：我不下。

A：勞駕 (láo jià excuse me)，我們下車。

3. Hiring a taxi or car

A：喂，出租汽車公司 (Chūzū Qìchē Gōngsī The Beijing
　　Taxicab Company) 嗎?

B：是啊，您哪兒?

A：我是鋼鐵學院⋯⋯

B：什麼? 請您再說一遍!

A：我是鋼鐵學院，我要一輛出租汽車*，去飛機場。

B：好，請等一下兒，車很快就到。

     *   *   *

(194,195)

1. The resultative complement

A resultative complement, expressed either by a verb or an adjective, indicates the result of an action." In "看見，開往，拿好，聽懂" and "坐錯", the resultative complements "見"，"往"，"懂" are verbs, and "好" and "錯" are adjectives.

A verb and its resultative complement are closely linked to each other and do not allow the insertion of another element between them. The aspect particle "了" and the object are usually placed after the complement.

Noun or pronoun	Verb	Verb or adjective (complement)	Particle "了"	Noun or pronoun	Particle "了"
他 我們 他	看 要鍛鍊 學	懂 好 會	了	這封中文信。 身體。 騎自行車	了。

Generally speaking, a verb followed by a resultative complement indicates that the action has concluded. Therefore "沒（有）" is used to make this type of structure negative and "…沒有" is used to form affirmative-negative sentence containing a structure of this type, e.g.

你今天看見他沒有？

我沒有看見他。

她學會開汽車了沒有？

她還沒學會呢。

2. "好" used as a resultative complement

The adjective "好" may serve as a resultative complement to indicate the desired state of an action, e.g.

我們一定要學好中文。

請大家坐好，現在上課了。

閱覽室的牆上寫著："請放好雜誌。"

The resultative complement "好" may sometimes also denote the completion of an action, e.g.

你的中式棉襖作好沒有？

這張畫兒還沒有畫好呢。

這條馬路什麼時候能修好？

七、練習 Exercises

1. Read aloud the following phrases:

開往香山　開往上海　飛往法國

往前跑　往裏開　往南拐（彎）　往上走

帶好東西　拿好車票　準備好行李

排好隊　整理好箱子　修好自行車

走錯了路　認錯了人　打錯了電話

坐錯了車　寫錯了字　唸錯了生詞

看見了　看懂了　說對了

聽見了　聽懂了　回答對了

剛下飛機　剛買票　剛起床　剛回家

剛下課　　剛上車　剛吃飯　剛開學

2. Choose the right word for the blanks:

聽　聽見

(1) A：你在作什麼呢？

B：我在＿＿音樂呢。

A：有人敲門，你＿＿了沒有？

B：我沒有＿＿。好，我去看一看。

(2) A：＿＿，外邊颳風了，你＿＿了嗎？

B：我早就＿＿了。

(3) A：這個故事你＿＿了嗎？

B：我＿＿過一遍了，還想再＿＿。

看　看見

(1) A：你去哪兒了？

B：我進城＿＿朋友了。

A：你＿＿古波和帕蘭卡沒有？他們倆也進城了。

B：我沒有＿＿他們。

(2) A：張大夫呢？

B：我＿＿他在公共汽車站等人呢。

(3) A：你＿＿那兒，那兒有一個公用電話。

B：在哪兒？我沒有＿＿。

A：你往左＿＿。

B：對，我＿＿了。

3. Fill in the blanks with a proper resultative complement:

(1) 我同學是上海人，他說上海話我不能聽＿＿。

(2) 這個練習不難，我們都作＿＿＿了。

(3) 明年他們就能看＿＿＿中文報了。

(4) 這本書不是老師給我們介紹的那本，我買＿＿＿了。

(5) 已經十點多了，明天的考試他還沒有準備＿＿＿呢。

(6) 昨天我剛開始學習滑冰，還沒有學＿＿＿呢。

4. Make two sentences with each of the following phrases:

(1) 修好　(2) 翻譯對　(3) 穿好　(4) 拿錯

(5) 辦好　(6) 聽懂

5. Translate the following sentences into Chinese:

(1) How do you write the character "帶", sir? （怎麼）

(2) He has just got up, and hasn't had his breakfast yet. （剛）

(3) Can you tell what direction this is? It's south. （方向）

(4) What's the Chinese for this word? （怎麼）

(5) How is he as a teacher of grammar? （講得怎麼樣）

(6) This jacket is too loose. Could you show me another one? （換）

(7) You run much faster than me. （跑）

6. Tell the story of the Reading Text with the help of the following pictures:

第三十九課

一、課　文

我們見到了你爸爸、媽媽

丁雲：

來信收到了。感謝你對我們的關心。

上星期我和古波去你家。路上我們坐錯了車，我們到你家的時候已經很晚了。我們見到了你爸爸、媽媽。你姐姐也帶著孩子小蘭回家看我們。

你爸爸工作很忙，上月車間里選舉，他當了車間主任。你媽媽說他比以前年輕了。他自己說，這叫"老驥伏櫪，志在千里"。我們都沒聽懂。你姐姐告訴我們："這是兩句古詩，爸爸的意思是：自己雖然老了，但是還要為實現四個現代化作更多的工作。"我覺得這句詩很好，就請你姐姐給我寫在本子上了。

你媽媽今年春天已經退休了。她身體很好，現在還能在街道上作一些工作呢。

小蘭真有意思，一看見我，她就指著牆上咱們的照片說：
"啊，照片上的阿姨來了。"

你們家的鄰居也都非常熱情。前邊的張大爺、對面的李大娘都來看我們，說我們是遠方的客人。

時間很晚了，我和古波要走，你媽媽一定要留我們吃飯。這時候小蘭說話了："叔叔、阿姨別走，聽我唱個歌兒。"她唱了一個《遠方的客人請你留下來》。六歲的小姑娘真聰明！她唱完歌兒，我們真不好意思走了。

跟你家裡人在一起，我和古波都覺得非常愉快。我們要永遠記住這一天。

好了，就寫到這兒吧。希望你常來信。

　祝

健康

　　　　　　　　　　　　　　　帕蘭卡

　　　　　　　　　　　　　　　十二月八日

二、生　詞

1. 對	duì	to; for
2. 關心	guānxīn	to care for; to be concerned with
3. 車間	chējiān	workshop
4. 選舉	xuǎnjǔ	to elect

5.主任	zhǔrèn	director; head
6.老驥伏櫪，	lǎojifúlì,	an old steed in the stable
志在千里	zhìzàiqiānlǐ	still aspires to gallop a thousand li, (fig.) old people may still cherish high aspirations
7.句	jù	a measure word, for sentences or lines of verse
8.意思	yìsi	meaning
9.雖然	suīrán	though; although
10.但是	dànshì	but
11.本子	běnzi	book; notebook
12.春天	chūntiān	spring
13.退休	tuìxiū	to retire
14.街道	jiēdào	street
15.一…就…	yī...jiù...	no sooner...than...; as soon as
16.阿姨	āyí	auntie
17.鄰居	línjū	neighbour
18.遠方	yuǎnfāng	distant place
19.客人	kèren	guest; visitor
20.留	liú	to remain; to ask somebody to stay
21.叔叔	shūshu	father's younger brother; uncle

22.聰明	cōngming	intelligent; bright
23.完	wán	to finish; to be over
24.不好意思	bù hǎoyìsi	to feel embarrassed; it is embarrassing (to do something)
25.愉快	yúkuài	happy; delighted
26.永遠	yǒngyuǎn	always; forever
27.記	jì	to remember; to bear in mind

專　名

小蘭	Xiǎolán	name of a person

補　充　詞

1.衣櫃	yīguì	wardrobe
2.書架	shūjià	bookshelf
3.師傅	shīfu	master; a qualified worker
4.壞	huài	(there is something) wrong with; out of order
5.手	shǒu	hand
6.條子	tiáozi	a short note; a slip of paper
7.關	guān	to close; to shut

三、閱讀短文

買　鞋

這是兩千(qiān thousand) 多年以前的一個故事。

有個人想買一雙鞋，他先量了量自己的腳(jiǎo foot)作好一個尺碼(chǐmǎ size)，可是走的時候，一著急就忘帶了。

到了商店，他才知道尺碼忘在家裡了。他對商店裡的人說：“我要買雙鞋，我已經量好了大小，可是尺碼忘帶了，我也沒有記住。我先回去拿尺碼再來買。”說完他就回家去拿。

等他拿了尺碼跑到商店的時候，商店已經關門 *了。來回走了很多路，還沒買到鞋，他很不高興。

他的一個朋友看見他沒買到鞋，就問他：“你給誰買鞋？”

他回答說：“給我自己買。”

他朋友說：“你給自己買鞋為什麼不用腳試 *，一定要拿尺碼呢？”

聽完他朋友的話，他說：“雖然用腳試也可以，但是我更相信(xiāngxìn to believe) 尺碼。”

四、注釋　Notes

1. "感謝你對我們的關心。"

"Thank you for being so much concerned about us."

The prepositional construction formed of "對" and its object may be used adjectivally (as in "對他的幫助", "對我們的希望"), or adverbially (as in "古波對我說", "他對大家都很熱情").

2. "老驥伏櫪，志在千里"

The two lines, quoted from Cao Cao's poem "A Tortoise May Live Long", are often used metaphorically to imply "never too old to work". Cao Cao (155 – 220 A.D.) was a statesman, strategist and poet who emerged towards the end of the Eastern Han Dynasty.

3. "現在還能在街道上作一些工作呢。"

"上" when used after a noun (uttered in a neutral tone) indicates range, sphere or limits, or a particular aspect of something, as in "街道上" (in the neighbourhood), "書上" (in the book).

The modal particle "呢" (2) often appears at the end of a declarative sentence, indicating confirmation or conviction, sometimes also conveying a sense of exaggeration.

Here "街道" stands for "neighbourhood committee", a non-governmental organization, in charge of after-school activities of the school-children, family planning, sanitation and hygiene of the neighbourhood, found in most of China's urban areas.

4. "前邊的張大爺，對面的李大娘都來看我們。"

In Beijing some of the old-styled single-storey houses have several court-yards. Here "前邊" means "the front courtyard", "對面" means "the house opposite" or "the house right in front".

5. "阿姨別走。"

"叔叔" and "阿姨" are forms of address used by children for male and female adults of about their parents's generation.

6. 《遠方的客人請你留下來》

"Please Don't Hurry Away, Guests From Afar" (title of a popular song)

7. "我們真不好意思走了。"

The expression "不好意思" means "shy" or "embarrassed", e.g. "大家一笑，她就不好意思了". Sometimes it also indicates unwillingness to do something out of politeness, e.g. "他很忙，我們不好意思再問他問題了". Its antonym "好意思" has a derogatory sense, and is seldom used.

五、替換與擴展　Substitution and Extension

（一）

1. 他們找到丁雲家了沒有？
   他們找到她家了。

| 見，她家的鄰居 |
| 聽，這個新聞 |
| 收，丁雲的信 |
| 學，第三十九課 |
| 買，唐山的茶具 |
| 拿，綢子棉襖 |

2. 你走到車站的時候已經很晚了嗎？
   我走到車站的時候已經十點多鐘了。

| 來，咖啡館 |
| 走，工廠 |
| 來，飛機場 |
| 回，學校 |
| 跑，醫務所 |

3. 那句詩你寫在哪兒了？
   那句詩我寫在本子上了。

那套明信片，	放，	桌子上
新衣服，	放，	箱子裏
今天的練習，	寫，	紙上
我的中山裝，	放，	衣櫃*裏
新雜誌，	放，	書架*上
齊白石的畫兒，	掛，	牆上

4. 他們唱完歌兒了沒有？
   他們還沒有唱完歌兒。

吃，	飯
學，	這本書
用，	本子
賽，	球
辦，	手續
參觀，	車間

5. 他家的地址你記住了沒有？
   我記住了。

這些生詞	這首詩的意思
車間的電話	那句成語
系主任的話	老師講的語法

6.他雖然<u>老了</u>，但是還願意在街道上作一些工作。

退休了　　身體不好
血壓很高　得了心臟病
文化不高　很忙

7.她一看見我就問：
　"你<u>接到</u>他的電話沒有?"

翻譯完，那本書
留住，那位客人
找到，你的筆
見到，你叔叔

(二)

1. At a bicycle service shop

A：師傅*，我的自行車要修一下兒。

B：車怎麼了 (what's wrong with the bike)?

A：車閘 (zhá hand brake) 壞*了。

B：放在那兒吧。

A：什麼時候能修好?

B：您明天來拿吧。

A：能不能快一點兒，我明天上午要用。

B：今天下午五點鐘，怎麼樣?

A：好，謝謝您。

2. Looking for something

    A：準備好了嗎? 咱們快走吧。

    B：好。——我的電影票呢?

    A：你放在哪兒了?

    B：我放在桌上了。你看見沒有?

    A：沒有。別著急，再找找。

       你手＊裏拿的是什麼?

    B：我的本子。啊，票在裏邊呢。

3. Looking for somebody

    A：你看見小張了嗎?

    B：沒有。吃完早飯以後，他就沒有回宿舍。

       你到閱覽室看看。

    A：我去過了，沒有找到。

    B：他會在哪兒呢?

    A：我留一個條子＊，請你交給他好嗎?

    B：好。這兒有紙。

＊   ＊   ＊

六、語法 Grammar

1. "到", "在" and "住" used as resultative complements

The verbs "到", "在" and "住" are often used as resultative complements.

When functioning as a resultative complement, "到" indicates the continuation of an action up to a certain point or a certain time, e.g.

我回到家就睡覺了。

從這兒騎到郵局要多長時間？

昨天晚上我看書看到十二點。

The resultative complement "到" also indicates the successful conclusion of an action. E.g.

他讓我等他的電話，半小時以後，我就接到他的電話了。

星期天我看見他又去書店了，不知道他買到那本書沒有。

上午我去找他，可是沒有找到他。

As a resultative complement, "在" denotes that a person or thing remains in a position as a result of an action. "在" must be followed by a word of locality which functions as the object of the verb. E.g.

那個孩子不願意坐在椅子上。

張大爺住在樓上。

你的行李放在車上了嗎？

The resultative complement "住" often indicates that something is fixed in a certain position as a result of a previous action. The verb "記" often goes with the resultative complement "住". "記住" means "to bear something in mind". E.g.

那個球他們接住了嗎？

他聽見後邊有人，就站住了。

這學期學過的漢字你都記住了嗎？

我記了一上午生詞，有的記住了，有的還沒有記住。

2. The construction "雖然…但是…"

"雖然…但是…" meaning "although...", is used to link two contradictory statements. "雖然" may go either before or after the subject of the first clause, while "但是" (or "可是") is always placed at the head of the second clause, e.g.

雖然外邊下著大雪，但是他還要騎車進城。

路上雖然很辛苦，但是他覺得很高興。

他雖然沒來過中國，可是對北京的情況了解得很多。

3. The construction "一…就…"

"一…就…" is used to connect two things that follow closely on one another.

我一放假就回國。

他一教，大家就會了。

Sometimes the first clause gives the condition, and the second gives the result, e.g.

他一著急，就寫錯了。

小蘭一唱歌，古波和帕蘭卡就不好意思走了。

七、練習 Exercises

1. Read aloud the following phrases:

見到親戚　　　回到宿舍　　　來到中國
走到學校　　　收到來信　　　復習到這兒

工作到十一點　談到這個問題

寫在本子上　　掛在牆上　　放在桌子上

收在箱子裏　　住在上海　　坐在車上

站在馬路上　　停在外邊　　拿在手＊裏

記住這件事兒　留住客人　　接住球

（人）站住　　（車）停住

喝完茶　　　　辦完事兒　　考完試

洗完澡　　　　看完病　　　照完相

看完這本書　　講完語法　　作完練習

整理完　　　　檢查完　　　翻譯完

對他說　　　　對大家很關心

對我的關心　　關心我們

2. Fill in each blank with a verb and a resultative complement:

   (1) A：你看見他的時候，他在作什麼？

   　　B：他在鍛鍊呢。

   　　A：現在他＿＿＿＿了沒有？

   　　B：我想他還沒有＿＿＿＿。

   (2) A：你們見到系主任的時候，他在作什麼？

   　　B：他在跟李老師談話呢。

   　　A：現在他們＿＿＿＿了沒有？

   　　B：我想他們還沒有＿＿＿＿。

   (3) A：昨天你到他們宿舍的時候，他們在作什麼？

   　　B：他們在找照片呢。

   　　A：他們＿＿＿＿了沒有？

B：他們說還沒有 _____ 。

(4) A：上午你怎麼沒有來?

B：我去火車站接我叔叔了。

A：你 _____ 了沒有?

B：他坐飛機來了，我 _____ 。

(5) A：你在唸課文嗎?

B：不，我在記生詞呢。

A：這一課的生詞你都 _____ 了嗎?

B：沒有， _____ 。

3. Translate the following into Chinese:

   (1) He couldn't find the place though he had tried to locate it the whole morning. （找到）

   (2) It was nearly twelve o'clock last Saturday night when the dance was over. （跳完）

   (3) He is going to stay in Beijing during the summer vacation. （留在）

   (4) Mr. Li, the teacher, is very concerned about his students. （關心）

   (5) Please hand in your exercise book tomorrow. （交）

   (6) What does this sentence mean? （意思）

   (7) This conductor is very warm towards the passengers. （對）

   (8) Although they didn't stay at her home for long, they had a very good time. （雖然…但是…）

   (9) How do you express this in Chinese? （怎麼）

   (10) Immediately after she received a letter from Palanka, Ding Yun wrote her a reply. （一…就…）

4. Read the following joke, then retell it:

   一位老人給遠方的兒子寫了一封信，說：「孩子，家裏要買一些東西，你給我寄點兒錢來吧。」

半個月以後，他收到他兒子的回信。信上寫著："爸爸，您要我寄錢的那封信，我沒有收到。"

5. Answer the questions according to the pictures:

(1)

古波住在哪兒？
他住在幾層？
他住在多少號？

(2)

老師站在哪兒？
學生坐在哪兒？
老師講完了課沒有？
學生回答完了老師的問題沒有？

(3)

昨天晚上看電影的時
候，你跟誰坐在一起？
他坐在幾排幾號？
坐在你們旁邊的是誰？

(4)

你的自行車放在哪兒？
車上放著什麼？
箱子裏放著什麼？

6. Pick a role and read the following dialogue:

（古波和帕蘭卡去看丁雲的爸爸、媽媽。丁雲姐姐的女兒小蘭站在門口，一見到帕蘭卡就非常高興地叫……）

小　蘭：媽媽，照片上的阿姨來了！

丁大娘：你們好！歡迎你們，請進！

帕蘭卡：我們坐錯車了，來晚了。

姐　姐：你們是遠方來的客人，請坐，別客氣。我給你們介紹一下兒，這是我爸爸、媽媽。這個小姑娘是我的女兒小蘭。我們雖然沒有見過面，但是我們在信裏面早就認識了。

帕蘭卡：大娘，您好。我們一到中國就想來看你們，總是沒找到一個合適的時間。

丁大爺：你們剛來，工作、學習都很忙。今天有空兒來我們家看看，我們非常高興。

古　波：您身體怎麼樣？工作很忙吧？

丁大娘：他身體很好。上月車間裏選舉，大家選他當車間主任。他比以前更忙了。我老了，已經從工廠退休了，只能在家裏給他們作作飯。

丁大爺：她是人老心不老，雖然退休了，但是還參加街道工作。為了國家早點兒實現四個現代化，現在我們這些老人都是"老驥伏櫪，志在千里"。

古　波："老驥伏櫪，志在千里"是什麼意思？

姐　姐：這是曹操的一句詩，意思是說，馬雖然老了，但是還想每天跑一千里路。

(228,229,230)

(lǐ a Chinese unit of length = 1/2 kilometre)

帕蘭卡：這兩句詩很有意思，請您給我寫在本子上吧。

丁大娘：今天我給你們作點兒中國菜，都是丁雲喜歡吃的。

古　波：別忙了，大娘。我們想早點兒回學校。

小　蘭：叔叔、阿姨你們別走，我給你們唱一個歌兒，好嗎？

帕蘭卡：太好了，你唱什麼歌兒？

小　蘭：這個歌兒叫《遠方的客人請你留下來》。……

古　波：唱得真好！

小　蘭：叔叔、阿姨你們還要走嗎？

帕蘭卡：我們不走了，我們就留在這兒聽你唱歌兒。

7. Write a letter in Chinese to your friend.

第四十課

復　習

一、課　文

運　動　會

"請運動員排好隊，運動會就要開始了，請運動員排好隊……"操場上正在廣播。

今天，語言學院大操場真漂亮。主席台上邊寫著"北京語言學院運動會"幾個大字，旁邊還有很多彩旗。

帕蘭卡看見古波還坐在那兒，她著急地說："古波，你聽到廣播了嗎？怎麼還不去？快去吧。"

古波是個運動員。冬天，他喜歡滑冰；夏天，他喜歡游泳。他跑一百米跑得非常快，足球也踢得不錯。帕蘭卡雖然自己不參加比賽，但是，她是一個熱情的觀眾，看比賽的時候她比運動員還激動呢！

操場中間，老師們正在打太極拳。帕蘭卡看見李老師也在裡邊，他打得很好，跟他上課一樣認真。打完太極拳，觀眾為他們熱烈地鼓掌。

男子一百米已經賽完了。帕蘭卡知道小張跑得也很好，他以前保持了學院男子一百米的記錄。帕蘭卡很想知道今天古波跑得有沒有小張快。這時，又廣播了：

"觀眾請注意：男子一百米第一名古波，十一秒一，打破了張華光十一秒三的院記錄；第二名張華光，十一秒二，也打破了他自己的記錄……"。

古波和小張正站在百米的終點那兒。小張高興地對古波說："今天你跑得好極了，祝賀你！"古波也笑著說："哪裡，我比你只快0.1秒，這個記錄你一定能打破。"

二、生　詞

1.運動會	yùndònghuì	sports meet
運動	yùndòng	to exercise (oneself); sport
2.運動員	yùndòngyuán	sportsman; player
3.操場	cāochǎng	sportsground
4.廣播	guǎngbō	to broadcast
5.主席台	zhǔxítái	rostrum; platform
主席	zhǔxí	chairman
6.彩旗	cǎiqí	coloured flag
旗子	qízi	flag; banner

7.比賽	bǐsài	to compete; competition; match
8.觀眾	guānzhòng	spectator; audience
9.激動	jīdòng	excited
10.打（拳）	dǎ (quán)	to do (shadowboxing)
11.太極拳	tàijíquán	a kind of traditional Chinese shadow-boxing
12.熱烈	rèliè	warm; enthusiastic
13.鼓掌	gǔ zhǎng	to applaud
14.男子	nánzǐ	man
15.保持	bǎochí	to keep; to retain
16.記錄	jìlù	record
17.名	míng	a measure word for people; a measure word, place (among winners)
18.秒	miǎo	second (of time)
19.打破	dǎ pò	to break
20.……極了	…jíle	extremely; exceedingly

三、注釋 Notes

1. "操場上正在廣播。"

"Someone was saying over the loudspeaker on the sports-ground."

2. "觀眾為他們熱烈地鼓掌。"

"The spectators applauded warmly for them."

3. "十一秒一。"

"11.1 seconds."

4. "你今天跑得好極了！"

"極了" often occurs after an adjective or a verb, meaning "extremely", e.g. "大極了", "難極了", "高興極了", "喜歡極了".

5. "我比你只快0.1秒。"

"0.1" is read as "零點一". A figure which is formed by a whole number and a fraction is read like this: The figures before the decimal point are read as integers; the decimal point is read as "點"; and the decimal is read as the figures are ordinarily read. "22.45", for example, is read as "二十二點四五", "0.02" as "零點零二".

四、看圖會話 Talk About These Pictures

Comparison

他有爸爸……

爸爸……

1 號樓比 2 號樓

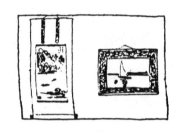

那種比這種……

小張比小王……

這張畫兒跟那張……

五、語法小結 A Brief Summary of Grammar

1. Four ways of making a comparison
(1) Using "跟…一樣"

這本詞典跟那本一樣。

他高興得跟孩子一樣。

他退休以後還跟以前一樣地關心車間的工作。

我要買一條跟你那條顏色一樣的裙子。

"跟……一樣" may function as a predicate, an adverbial modifier, an adjective modifier or a complement.

(2) Using "有"

這個姑娘快有她媽媽高了。

這種花兒沒有那種好看。

(3) Using "更" or "最"

他打太極拳打得不錯，他哥哥打得更好。

這次咱們班誰考試成績最好?

Note that the above-mentioned methods are used to express comparison in general terms, without stating the specific differences.

(4) Using "比"

小張修自行車比我修得好。

那種汽車的質量不比這種好。

我們學校的操場比他們的大得多。

這種綢子比那種每米便宜五塊錢。

"比" used in a comparison may state specific differences.

2. The modal particles "吧", "呢" and "了"

"吧"

(1) "吧" softens the tone when used in sentences of request, advice or command.

請吧。

大夫，請給我量量血壓吧。

再吃點兒吧。

(2) "吧" indicates uncertainty.

我是丁雲，你是帕蘭卡吧?

你參加一百米比賽了吧?

今天星期五吧?

"呢"

(1) "呢" softens the tone in an interrogative sentence.

我們在哪兒停車呢?

咱們坐不坐公共汽車呢?

(2) "呢" is used in a declarative sentence to emphasize the truth of a statement.

她現在還能在街道上作一些工作呢。

還早呢，再玩兒玩兒吧。

(3) "呢" helps form a question.

我很好，你呢？

古波呢？

(4) "呢" indicates an action that is progressing or continuous.

他們唱歌呢。

外邊下著雨呢。

"了"

(1) "了" indicates that something has already occurred.

我去中國大使館辦簽證了。

他們的車間主任已經退休了。

這個工廠的生產比以前提高了。

(2) "了" suggests advice or warning.

別難過了，明年我們去中國看他們。

別留他了，他還有事情呢。

這是誰的茶碗？別拿錯了。

(3) "了" indicates changed circumstances.

現在是秋天了。樹上的葉子都紅了。

他願意參加運動會了。

她一說，小姑娘就不哭了。

前邊要拐彎了，請大家坐好。

(243,244)

六、練習 Exercises

1. Fill one character in each blank to form words or phrases:

上：上＿＿＿　上＿＿＿　上＿＿＿　上＿＿＿　上＿＿＿　上＿＿＿　上＿＿＿

下：下＿＿＿　下＿＿＿　下＿＿＿　下＿＿＿　下＿＿＿　下＿＿＿　下＿＿＿　下＿＿＿

開：開＿＿＿　開＿＿＿　開＿＿＿　開＿＿＿

打：打＿＿＿　打＿＿＿　打＿＿＿

接：接＿＿＿　接＿＿＿　接＿＿＿　接＿＿＿

看：看＿＿＿　看＿＿＿　看＿＿＿　看＿＿＿　看＿＿＿　看＿＿＿　看＿＿＿

員：＿＿＿員＿＿＿員＿＿＿員＿＿＿員＿＿＿員＿＿＿

子：＿＿＿子＿＿＿子＿＿＿子＿＿＿子＿＿＿子＿＿＿子＿＿＿子＿＿＿

＿＿＿子＿＿＿子＿＿＿子＿＿＿子＿＿＿子＿＿＿子＿＿＿子＿＿＿

2. Translate the following into Chinese:

   (1)   This workshop is bigger than that one.

   (2)   There are a much smaller number of students in the Languages Institute than in the Iron and Steel Engineering Institute.

   (3)   Palanka cannot ride a bike as fast as Gubo does.

   (4)   This suit is 12 yuan cheaper than that one, and the quality of this suit is not as good as that one.

   (5)   Is the production of this factory increasing as fast as that factory?

   (6)   The colour of this car is the same as that one.

   (7)   Is the story you heard the same as the one I told you?

   (8)   He learned as many new words as you have, but he doesn't remember as many as you do.

   (9)   Xiao Wang does *taijiquan* (shadowboxing) best in our class.

  (10)   I prefer Beijing opera.

3. Fill in the blanks in the following dialogues with the modal particle "吧", "呢" or "了":

(1) A：你下星期能看完這本書____?

　　B：我這星期就能看完這本書____。

(2) A：我不想今天去____。

　　B：我們還是明天一起去____。

(3) A：他們在看病____?

　　B：不，他們檢查身體____。

(4) A：咱們聽什麼?

　　B：咱們聽新聞廣播____。

(5) A：聽，颶風____。

　　B：還下著雨____。

4. Fill in the blanks in the following dialogues with a proper resultative complement:

A：運動會開始了沒有?

B：剛開始，太極拳已經打____了。我星期二給你的信，你收____了嗎?

A：收____了。知道你們今天開運動會，我很想來看。一上____課，我就騎車來了。只用了半個小時就騎____了。

B：你騎得真快。你吃了午飯沒有?

A：沒有，我看____商店裏有麵包就買了兩個。

B：你真是一位好觀眾。咱們就站____這兒看吧?

A：坐____主席台旁邊比這兒好。

B：好吧。我們一起去。

A：你看，百米（比）賽已經開始了，古波和小張快跑＿＿
終點了。

5. Describe the pictures, then read the short passage that follows:

我和帕蘭卡…　　…小張在窗口買票　　進電影院…

她幫助我們…　　這個片子很長　　…小張回家了

　　我和帕蘭卡七點一刻走到電影院（diànyǐngyuàn cinema）的
時候，看見小張站在窗口買票。我們站住問他："買到票了
沒有？"他很高興地告訴我們："買到了七點半的電影票。"
進電影院的時候，我們準備好了票，給檢查票的同志看了看，
她幫助我們找到了座位。我們三個人坐在一起。這個電影很
長，演到九點半。看完電影，小張就回家了。我和帕蘭卡十
點半回到了學校。

6. Correct the following sentences:

　　(1) 新馬路比舊馬路最長。

　　(2) 比那個公園，這個公園大一點兒。

(3) 今天晚上我完了練習就看電視。

(4) 這套茶具一樣跟那套。

(5) 他聽有人敲門。

(6) 今天比昨天很冷。

(7) 我看了他在那兒。

(8) 他這次考試成績比她不高。

(9) 哥哥比妹妹三歲大。

(10) 她爸爸希望他們學中文好。

七、語音語調 Pronunciation and Intonation

1. Rhythm of phrases and long sentences

(1) Rhythm of phrases

A phrase (or word-group) is a meaning unit formed of a number of syllables. A phrase forming part of a long sentence normally makes up one beat. A phrase with many syllables should be uttered rapidly. A phrase containing 4—5 Chinese characters can usually be divided into two groups, each of which takes the same length of time. E.g.

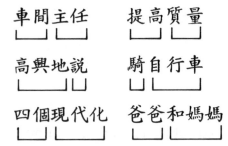

(2) Rhythm of long sentences

A long sentence may be divided into a number of phrases according to their grammatical relationships, then read as each phrase should be read. A phrase with more syllables should be uttered a little more quickly than those with fewer syllables, so that the whole sentence will be a marked rhythmical utterance, bringing out the meaning clearly. E.g.

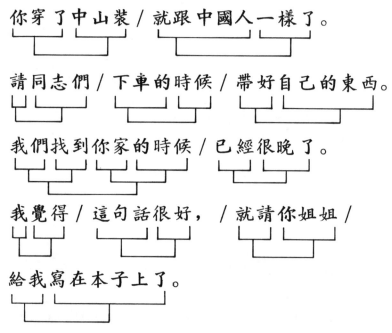

2. Sense group stress (7)

(1) In Subject + Prepositional structure (adverbial adjunct) + Verb construction, the adverbial adjunct is usually stressed, the preposition is not stressed but the nouns or pronouns that follow are normally stressed. E.g.

百貨大樓比這兒大。

景德鎮的瓷器比玉白。

他比以前年輕了。

(2) In Subject + Prepositional structure (adverbial adjunct) + Verb + Object construction, the object is normally stressed. If the sentence is a long one, it may be divided into two sense groups, and a short pause may be made after the prepositional structure. The objects of the preposition and the verb are both stressed. E.g.

古波比帕蘭卡／注意語法。

我朋友比我了解情況。

他們在平安里下車。

(3) In Subject + Prepositional structure (the adverbial adjunct) + Verb + Complement construction, the complement is usually stressed. If the sentence is a long one, it may be divided into several sense groups. The noun and the pronoun after the preposition and the complement may all be stressed. E.g.

他比我小三歲。

古波比帕蘭卡／多花七十多塊錢。

你比小張／跑得快。

(4) Subject + Verb + Complement construction, the complement is normally stressed. E.g.

你聽懂了嗎?

——我聽懂了。

你沒聽錯嗎?

——我沒聽錯。

(5) In Subject + Verb + Complement + Object construction, the object is generally stressed. E.g.

他看懂了這封中文信。

她唱完歌兒了。

我們要永遠記住這一天。

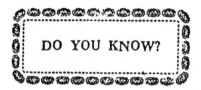

China's Administrative Divisions

China has three administrative levels: provinces (including municipalities directly under the central government and autonomous regions), counties and people's communes. There are 30 divisions on the provincial level: 22 provinces, 5 autonomous regions and 3 municipalities.

Name		Abbreviation		Seat of the provincial capital	
北京市	Beijing Shi	京	Jing		
上海市	Shanghai Shi	滬	Hu		
天津市	Tianjin Shi	津	Jin		
河北省	Hebei Sheng	冀	Ji	石家莊市	Shijiazhuang Shi
山西省	Shanxi Sheng	晉	Jin	太原市	Taiyuan Shi
內蒙古自治區 Nei Monggol Zizhiqu		內蒙古 Nei Monggol		呼和浩特市	Huhehaote Shi
遼寧省 Liaoning Sheng		遼	Liao	瀋陽市	Shenyang Shi
吉林省	Jilin Sheng	吉	Ji	長春市	Changchun Shi
黑龍江省 Heilongjiang Sheng		黑	Hei	哈爾濱市	Ha erbin Shi
山東省 Shandong Sheng		魯	Lu	濟南市	Jinan Shi
河南省 Henan Sheng		豫	Yu	鄭州市	Zhengzhou Shi

江蘇省 Jiangsu Sheng	蘇 Su	南京市 Nanjing Shi
安徽省 Anhui Sheng	皖 Wan	合肥市 Hefei Shi
浙江省 Zhejiang Sheng	浙 Zhe	杭州市 Hangzhou Shi
江西省 Jiangxi Sheng	贛 Gan	南昌市 Nanchang Shi
福建省 Fujian Sheng	閩 Min	福州市 Fuzhou Shi
臺灣省 Taiwan Sheng	臺 Tai	
湖北省 Hubei Sheng	鄂 E	武漢市 Wuhan Shi
湖南省 Hunan Sheng	湘 Xiang	長沙市 Changsha Shi
廣東省 Guangdong Sheng	粤 Yue	廣州市 Guangzhou Shi
廣西壯族自治區 Guangxi Zhuangzu Zizhiqu	桂 Gui	南寧市 Nanning Shi
甘肅省 Gansu Sheng	甘 Gan 或 隴 Long	蘭州市 Lanzhou Shi
青海省 Qinghai Sheng	青 Qing	西寧市 Xining Shi
寧夏回族自治區 Ningxia Huizu Zizhiqu	寧 Ning	銀川市 Yinchuan Shi
陝西省 Shanxi Sheng	陝 Shan	西安市 Xi an Shi
新疆維吾爾自治區 Xinjiang Uygur Zizhiqu	新 Xin	烏魯木齊市 Urumqi Shi
四川省 Sichuan Sheng	川 Chuan 或 蜀 Shu	成都市 Chengtu Shi
貴州省 Guizhou Sheng	貴 Gui 或 黔 Qian	貴陽市 Guiyang Shi
雲南省 Yunnan Sheng	雲 Yun 或 滇 Dian	昆明市 Kunming Shi
西藏自治區 Xizang Zizhiqu	藏 Zang	拉薩市 Lhasa Shi

(257,258)

第四十一課

一、課　文

我給你們帶來一位嚮導

（古波、帕蘭卡在景山公園裡。帕蘭卡看見張
　華光正在公園門口買票）

帕蘭卡：喂，小張，我們在這兒呢。

張華光：我們就來。（對哥哥）哥哥，他們已經進去了，咱們
　　　　也進去吧。

（他們走進公園）

張華光：對不起，我們來晚了。

帕蘭卡：沒關係。我和古波在外邊等了一會兒，古波著急，我
　　　　們就先進來了。

張華光：這是我哥哥，張華明。

帕蘭卡：你好。

張華明：你好。

張華光：古波呢？

帕蘭卡：他像孩子一樣，看見那個亭子好看，就上山去了。

古　波：誰是孩子？我來了。（對張華明）你好。小張，你怎麼現在才來？

張華光：今天車真擠。我起床以後洗了洗衣服，八點就從家裡出來了，在路上花了一個多小時才到這兒。

帕蘭卡：是啊，今天外邊人多極了。

張華明：星期天大家都喜歡到公園來玩兒，或者到商店去買東西。

張華光：今天我給你們帶來一位嚮導，我哥哥是汽車司機，他對北京很了解，讓他給咱們好好兒介紹介紹。

古　波：小張，你想得真週到。謝謝你們。

張華明：不謝。今天我休息，也想到公園來玩兒。我們從西邊上山吧。這兒從前是皇帝的花園，也是北京城最高的地方。站在景山上，北京的街道、建築都看得清清楚楚。要是天氣好，就能看得更遠。

古　波：下邊是故宮嗎？

張華明：對。

帕蘭卡：最前邊的那個高高的建築是什麼？

張華明：那是天安門。你看見前邊的廣場嗎？那就是天安門廣場。

古　波：這個地方美極了。帕蘭卡，你帶照相機來了嗎？快過來給我們照一張。

帕蘭卡：好。你們就站在那兒。

⋯⋯⋯⋯⋯⋯

張華明：我們從東邊下去，走到山脚下就能看見崇禎皇帝吊死
　　　　的地方。

帕蘭卡：皇帝吊死的地方？我聽說有一本小說寫到了這個皇帝
　　　　的故事。

張華光：對，這本小說叫《李自成》。你們看過嗎？

古　波：我還沒看過。

張華光：你們應該看看這本小說。這本書可以幫助你們了解中
　　　　國歷史。一會兒我們從東門出去吧。

二、生　詞

1.嚮導	xiàngdǎo	guide
2.門口	ménkǒu	doorway; entrance
3.對不起	duì bu qǐ	(I'm) sorry
4.沒關係	méi guānxi	it doesn't matter
5.一會兒	yìhuìr	a little while
6.亭子	tíngzi	pavilion
7.山	shān	hill; mountain
8.才	cái	only just; not... until...

9. 擠	jǐ	crowded; to squeeze
10. 洗	xǐ	to wash
11. 司機	sījī	driver
12. 週到	zhōudào	thoughtful; considerate
13. 西邊	xībiān	west; western part
14. 皇帝	huángdì	emperor
15. 建築	jiànzhù	building; to build; to construct
16. 清楚	qīngchu	clear
17. 要是	yàoshi	if
18. 廣場	guǎngchǎng	square
19. 美	měi	beautiful
20. 照相機	zhàoxiàngjī	camera
21. 過	guò	to come over; to pass by
22. 腳	jiǎo	foot
23. 吊	diào	to hang
24. 死	sǐ	to die
25. 聽説	tīng shuō	it is said that
26. 小説	xiǎoshuō	novel; short story
27. 出	chū	to come out; to go out

專　名

1.景山公園	Jǐngshān Gōngyuán	name of a park in Beijing
2.景山	Jǐngshān	name of a hill in Jingshan park
3.張華明	Zhāng Huámíng	name of a person
4.故宮	Gùgōng	the Imperial Palace
5.天安門廣場	Tiān'ānmén Guǎngchǎng	Tiananmen Square
6.崇禎	Chóngzhēn	Emperor Chongzhen
7.李自成	Lǐ Zìchéng	name of a person

補　充　詞

1.售票處	shòupiàochù	ticket office; booking office
2.講解員	jiǎngjiěyuán	guide
3.丟	diū	to lose
4.廣播室	guǎngbōshì	broadcasting room
5.摩托車	mótuōchē	motorcycle
6.旅館	lǚguǎn	hotel
7.廣播員	guǎngbōyuán	radio (or wire-broadcasting) announcer

三、閱讀短文

一封電報

(264,265,272)

一天晚上，已經快八點了。一輛摩托車*開到人民旅館*門口。一會兒，從門口進來一個穿綠衣服的人。他是郵局送電報 (diànbào, telegram) 的老高同志。

　　老高一進門就問旅館的服務員*：“李雲亭同志住在幾號房間？這兒有他的電報。”

　　服務員接過電報看了看説：“啊！李雲亭剛走。他要坐晚上八點半的火車回西安 (Xī'ān, name of a city) 去。他等電報等到七點多鐘才離開這兒。你要是早來半個小時，他就能收到這封電報了。”

　　老高一看錶，剛過八點，離開車的時間還有二十多分鐘。他想了想，又問服務員：“這個同志穿的是什麼衣服？”

　　“灰中山裝。他跟我一樣高，瘦瘦的……”。

　　“謝謝你，再見！”老高騎上摩托車*就往火車站開去。

　　車站裡人多極了，到哪兒去找李雲亭呢？這時，老高同志聽到廣播説：“開往西安的 179 次車，還有十分鐘就要開車了。……”他高興地説：“對！去找車站廣播室*。”

　　“同志，我是郵局送電報的。這兒有一封電報，要找一個人……請您廣播一下兒。”

　　“好，我現在就廣播。”廣播員説，“去西安的李雲亭同志，請你快到廣播室*來一下兒，有你的電報……”

　　廣播員*廣播了兩遍。

老高站在廣播*室門口，著急地等著。一會兒，一個瘦瘦的穿灰中山裝的人跑來了。老高問他：「您是李雲亭同志嗎？」

「是啊，我是李雲亭。」

「這是您的電報，請在這兒寫上您的名字。」

李雲亭看完電報，激動地對老高說：「這是工廠給我來的電報，讓我先留在這兒，還有事兒要辦。同志，太感謝您了！」

「不用謝，再見！」

四、注釋　Notes

1. "他像孩子一樣。"

The phrase "像…一樣" may be used as a predicate, an adjective modifier or an adverbial modifier to express comparison.

2. "小張，你怎麼現在才來?"

Unlike "就", the adverb "才" indicates that the action referred to did not occur as soon, as quickly or as smoothly as expected, e.g. "這個故事我聽了三遍才聽懂。"

3. "走到山脚下就能看見崇禎皇帝吊死的地方。"

"When we get to the foot of the hill, we can see the place where Emperor Chongzhen hanged himself."

Chongzhen, the last Emperor of the Ming Dynasty, hanged himself on a tree on Jingshan Hill in 1644 when the peasant uprising troops under Li Zicheng broke into the city of Beijing.

4. "我聽說有一本小說寫到了這個皇帝的故事。"

When it is combined with verbs such as "說", "談", "寫" or "問" etc. as a resultative complement, "到" means "with regard to" or "concerning", e.g. "說到這件事兒", "談到學校的情況", "問到這個問題".

5. "這本小說叫《李自成》。"

"李自成" is the title of a five-volume novel, written by Yao Xueyin. It describes the peasant uprising in the last years of the Ming Dynasty. The first two volumes were published in 1963, 1976 respectively.

6. "一會兒我們從東門出去吧。"

"We'll go out through the east gate when l we leave."

Here "一會兒" means "in a moment" or "a few minutes later".

五、替換與擴展 Substitution and Extension

(一)

1. 你們在<u>公園外邊</u>等我了吧?
   我們等了你一會兒,就先<u>進</u>來了。

學校裏,	出
山腳下,	上
操場上,	回
亭子裏,	下
售票處*,	過

2. 你看見他們了嗎?
   他們在<u>山上</u>,你快<u>上</u>去吧。

樓下,	下
房間裏,	進
門口,	出
公園裏,	進
廣場上,	過

3. 小張在嗎?
   不在,他<u>回</u>家<u>去</u>了。

回,	宿舍
進,	城
上,	主席台
下,	樓
到,	北海

4. 你們帶照相機來了嗎?
   我們沒帶照相機來。

| 語法書 | 本子 |
| 詞典 | 行李 |

5. 你給他寄去了什麼?
   我給他寄去了二十塊錢。

送，	幾本小說
帶，	一些點心
寄，	一套茶具

6. 我給你們帶來了一位嚮導。
   太好了，你想得真週到。

找，	一位司機
送，	運動會的票
買，	天安門廣場的圖片
拿，	吃的東西
請，	講解員 *

7. 你明天出去嗎?
   要是天氣好我就出去。

回來，	不下雨
到機場去，	有時間
進城去，	洗完衣服
上香山去，	接到我朋友的電話

(268,269)

1. Calling somebody over the loudspeaker

　　語言學院的古波同學請注意：聽到廣播以後，請到門口去。有人找您。

　　　　　*　　　　　*　　　　　*

　　哪位同志丟*了小孩兒，請到廣播室*來。

2. Calling on somebody

　　A：請問，王主任在嗎？

　　B：在。他在裏邊等您呢，請進去吧。

　　A：（敲門）可以進來嗎？

　　C：啊，你來了，快進來吧。

　　　　……

　　A：你忙吧，我該回去了。

　　C：有什麼問題，你再來找我。

　　A：謝謝。你不要出來了。

　　C：好，我不送了。慢慢兒走。

3. Making a suggestion

　　A：今天天氣真好，下午我們出去走走，怎麼樣？

　　B：好啊，咱們到哪兒去呢？

　　A：咱們進城去吧。聽説最近書店裏有一些新小説。

　　B：城裏太擠，還是到公園去吧。

　　A：也好。可是不能回來得太晚，晚上我有事兒。

4. Bringing something to somebody

　　A：她要的小説《李自成》，你買來了沒有？

B：買來了。可是我沒有帶來，放在家裏了。明天我給
你送來吧。

A：不用了。還是我去拿吧。明天下午我進城給她送去。

＊　　　＊　　　＊

六、語法　Grammar

1.　The simple directional complement

"來" or "去" are often used after certain verbs to show the direction
of a movement.　Modifiers of this type are known as "simple directional
complements".　If the movement proceeds toward the speaker or the thing
referred to, "來" is used.　If the movement proceeds away from the speaker,
"去" is used, e.g.

下雨了，你們都進來吧。(說話人在裡邊)

李老師不在家，他出去了。(說話人在家裡)

When a verb having a simple directional complement is followed by an
object and when the object is expressed by a noun or a phrase of locality,
it should be placed between the verb and the complement.　In a sentence of
this kind, the verb must not be followed by the aspect particle "了", though
it may end with the modal particle "了", to indicate that the action referred
to has already taken place.

— 177 —

(271,274,275)

Noun or pronoun	Adverb	Verb	Noun (of locality)	"來" or "去"	Particle
我 他 大夫	常常 快 沒有	到 進 回 下	上海 屋裏 宿舍 樓	去。 來 去。 來	吧。 了。

When the object is expressed by a word other than a noun or phrase of locality, it is also placed between the verb and the complement, e.g.

Noun or pronoun	Adverb	Verb	Particle	Noun or pronoun	"來" or "去"	Particle
我 他 我們	沒有	想帶 打 寄	了	照相機 電話 一封信	去。 來 去。	嗎?

Objects of this type may also follow the complement, especially when the action referred to has already been accomplished, e.g.

Noun or pronoun	Adverb	Verb	"來" or "去"	Particle	Noun or pronoun
我 他 我們	沒有	帶 打 寄	去 來 去	了 了	照相機。 電話。 一封信。

As the above two tables show, the aspect particle "了" may be used to indicate that the action has concluded when the object is not a noun or a phrase of locality. "了" is placed between the verb and the object, if the verb is separated from the directional complement by the object. "了" is placed between the complement and the object if the verb is immediately followed by the directional complement.

2. Repetition of adjectives

Certain types of adjectives may be repeated. In spoken Chinese, the second syllable of a repeated monosyllabic adjective is often pronounced in the first tone, and becomes retroflexed, e.g. "好好兒", "慢慢兒". In the case of dissyllabic adjectives, they are duplicated in the form of AABB, with the fourth syllable stressed, e.g. "清清楚楚", "高高興興".

When repeated, adjectives often function as adverbial modifiers, indicating a greater degree of the attribute denoted. As an adverbial modifier, a repeated monosyllabic adjective is not normally followed by "地", but "地" is generally needed after a repeated dissyllabic adjective. When functioning as complements or attributive modifiers, repeated forms of adjectives are usually more descriptive, often expressing emotions such as pleasure or admiration. When used as attributive modifiers, repeated adjectives are usually followed by "的", e.g.

(276,277)

別著急，慢慢兒唸。

孩子們高高興興地到學校去了。

他是個很好的嚮導，給我們介紹得清清楚楚。

他女兒有一雙大大的眼睛，非常像她媽媽。

Note that not all adjectives may be duplicated. It is wrong, for instance, to say "錯錯", "聰聰明明", "熱熱烈烈".

3. The construction "要是…就…"

The adverb "就" may be used to link what follows with the foregoing sentence in a concluding remark. A conjunction is usually used in the preceding clause to form a conjunctive phrase with "就" denoting condition, purpose and reason, etc. The first part of a sentence containing "要是…就…" usually expresses condition, e.g.

要是你每天都鍛鍊，你的身體就會很健康。

他要是不來，我們就去找他。

It is also possible for "就" to be used without conjunction in the foregoing part, e.g.

古波著急，我們就先進來了。

他沒有聽懂，老師就又講了一遍。

七、練習 Exercises

1. Read aloud the following phrases:

等一會兒　想一會兒　騎一會兒

站一會兒　洗一會兒　檢查了一會兒

研究了一會兒　了解了一會兒　廣播了一會兒

進來　出去　上來　下去　回來　過去

拿去了一套茶具　帶來了一封信

送去了幾本小説　打來了一個電話

找了一位司機來　寄了五十塊錢去

到北京來了　　　　　下樓去了

高高的　長長的　瘦瘦的　慢慢的　薄薄的

白白的　早早的　短短的　遠遠的　紅紅的

辛辛苦苦的　認認真真的　清清楚楚的

2. Fill in the blanks with "來" or "去" according to the speaker's position:

(1) 他們已經進 ＿＿＿ 了。（說話人在外邊）

(2) 請大家從東門出 ＿＿＿ 吧，汽車在門口等你們。（說話人在裏邊）

(3) 古波跟他的朋友從景山下 ＿＿＿ 了。（說話人在山下）

(4) 小張星期六吃了晚飯以後就回家 ＿＿＿ 了。（說話人在學校）

(5) 我的朋友昨天給我送 ＿＿＿ 了三個本子。

3. Complete the following sentences with the adverb "就":

Example:　他等了你半天了，你還沒回來，他 ＿＿＿＿＿＿ 。

　　　　　→他等了你半天了，你還沒回來，他就走了。

(1) 你先下樓去等我，我一會兒 ＿＿＿＿＿＿ 。

(2) 古波和帕蘭卡剛下了飛機，小張 ＿＿＿＿＿＿ 。

(3) 她覺得今天有點兒熱，她 ＿＿＿＿＿＿ 。

(4) 他聽説書店有《李自成》這本小説，他 ＿＿＿＿＿＿ 。

(5) 要是古波聽懂了老大爺的話，他們 ＿＿＿＿＿＿ 。

　　　　　(279,280,281)

(6) 要是商店裏有綢面兒的棉襖，帕蘭卡＿＿＿＿＿＿＿。

4. Translate the following into Chinese:

(1) Sorry, I forgot all about it. （對不起）

(2) Excuse me, but can I make a phone call? （對不起）

(3) He came to the sportsground at eight o'clock, though the sports meet wouldn't begin until nine. （才，就）

(4) It is only today that I have the chance to visit this building, though I have always heard about it. （就，才）

(5) Xiao Zhang is not in. He has just gone out, but will be back in a minute. （出去，回來）

(6) I'm not going in, but could you tell him that we are going to visit the Palace Museum tomorrow? （進去，到…去）

(7) Last month my brother bought me two Chinese novels. I've sent one to my sister. （買來，送去）

(8) If buses are too crowded, we'll go by bike. （要是…就…）

5. Put the underlined adjectives into reduplicated forms:

Example: 他們很高興地上山去了。

　　　　→他們高高興興地上山去了。

(1) 上次他來晚了，很不好意思。今天他很早地來到公園門口。

(2) 她非常客氣地對他説：“對不起，我今天很忙。”

(3) 那本小説的故事我現在還記得很清楚。

(4) 他今天穿得很漂亮。

(5) 他每天都認真地打太極拳。

6. Describe the pictures:

A：水真好，
　　你們快⋯
B：⋯

A：這兒好看極了，
　　快⋯
B：⋯

A：裏面有什麼？
　　我們⋯
B：⋯

A：我們從西邊⋯

B：從東邊⋯

第四十二課

一、課　文

今天的照片洗不好了

（在天安門前）

帕蘭卡：古波，這個石獅子像真的一樣。

古　波：來，在這兒照張相。

帕蘭卡：天安門照得上照不上？

古　波：照得上。還能照得上那個……帕蘭卡，你知道那叫什麼？

男　孩：（在旁邊回答）那叫華表。

帕蘭卡：啊，小朋友，謝謝你。這個漂亮的小姑娘是你妹妹嗎？

男　孩：是。爺爺帶我們來玩兒，他去買冰棍兒了。

女　孩：阿姨好，叔叔好！

帕蘭卡：你好。過來，跟阿姨一起照張相吧。

古　波：笑一笑。好。

（老大爺走來）

老大爺：小紅、小冬，你們都在這兒！我剛走開，就找不到你們了。快來吃冰棍兒。

古　波：老大爺，您好！

老大爺：你們好。到天安門來照相，是嗎？

帕蘭卡：是啊，這兒很美。

老大爺：你們看：天安門、華表、石獅子都是典型的中國古典建築——我的話你們都聽得懂嗎？

古　波：聽得懂。老大爺，天安門有多高？

老大爺：天安門有三十多米高。這個廣場站得下一百萬人。中間是人民英雄紀念碑，上邊有毛主席寫的字，你們看得見嗎？

帕蘭卡：看得見。

老大爺：廣場西邊的人民大會堂、東邊的中國歷史博物館，這些都是中國最有名的現代建築。

古　波：老大爺，您對建築藝術很有研究啊！

老大爺：哪裡，我以前是建築工人。1959年修建人民大會堂，我也參加了。裡邊的大禮堂有七十六米寬、六十米長，一共有三層，每層都坐得下幾千人。這麼大的建築，那時候只用了十個月就完成了。

帕蘭卡：真快！您今年多大歲數了？身體真好啊！

老大爺：我今年六十九歲，已經退休了。現在幹不了重活兒，

　　　　路也走不動了，但是眼睛還看得清楚，耳朵也聽得見

　　　　。身體好的時候，我就去工地看看。

女　孩：我爺爺是工地顧問，家裡還有獎狀呢。

古　波：好，今天的照片洗好了，可以掛在爺爺的獎狀旁邊。

女　孩：今天的照片洗不好了。

古　波：為什麼呢？

女　孩：您給我們照相的時候沒拿下鏡頭蓋兒。

二、生　詞

1.洗（照片）	xǐ (zhàopiàn)	to develop (a film)
2.石（頭）	shí (tou)	stone; rock
3.獅子	shīzi	lion
4.華表	huábiǎo	marble pillar (an ornamental column erected in front of palaces, tombs, etc.)
5.爺爺	yéye	grandpa
6.冰棍兒	bīnggùnr	ice-lolly; ice-sucker
7.典型	diǎnxíng	typical; model
8.萬	wàn	ten thousand
9.中間	zhōngjiān	centre; middle
10.藝術	yìshù	art

(289,290)

11.修建	xiūjiàn	to build; to construct
12.禮堂	lǐtáng	assembly hall; auditorium
13.寬	kuān	wide
14.千	qiān	thousand
15.這麼	zhème	so; such
16.完成	wánchéng	to complete; to finish
17.歲數	suìshu	age
18.幹	gàn	to work; to do
19.了	liǎo	to end up
20.重	zhòng	heavy
21.活兒	huór	work; job
22.動	dòng	to move
23.工地	gōngdì	construction site
24.顧問	gùwèn	adviser
25.獎狀	jiǎngzhuàng	certificate of merit
26.鏡頭	jìngtóu	camera lens
27.蓋兒	gàir	cover; lid

專　名

1.小紅	Xiǎohóng	name of a child
2.小冬	Xiǎodōng	name of a child

3.人民英雄	Rénmín Yīngxióng	Monument to the People's
紀念碑	Jìniànbēi	Heroes
4.毛主席	Máo Zhǔxí	Chairman Mao
5.人民大會堂	Rénmín Dàhuìtáng	Great Hall of the People
6.中國歷史博	Zhōngguó Lìshǐ	Museum of Chinese
物館	Bówùguǎn	History

補　充　詞

1.搬	bān	to move; to take away
2.尺	chǐ	a unit of length (=1/3 metre)
3.平方米	píngfāngmǐ	square metre
4.公斤	gōngjīn	kilogram (kg.)
5.方便	fāngbiàn	convenient; to make it convenient for
6.海	hǎi	sea
7.可笑	kěxiào	ridiculous; laughable

三、閱讀短文

愚 公 移 山

古時候有位老人，名字叫愚公 (Yúgōng the Foolish Old Man)，快九十歲了。他家的門口有兩座 (zuò a measure word)大山，一家人出來進去很不方便*。

一天，愚公對家裡人説：“這兩座山在咱們家的門口，太不方便了。咱們移(yí to remove)　走這兩座山，好不好？”

他的兒子(érzi son)、孫子(sūnzi grandson)　一聽，都説：“您説得對，咱們明天就開始幹！”他妻子(qīzi wife)覺得搬山太難了，她説：“你們知道這兩座山有多高嗎？這麼大的山你們怎麼搬得動？哪兒放得下這麼多石頭呢？”

大家説：“只要我們一起努力幹，就一定搬得了這兩座山。山上的石頭我們可以放到海裡去。”

第二天，愚公帶著一家人開始搬山了。鄰居有個孩子，聽説要搬山，也高高興興地跟他們一起去了。他們不怕颱風，不怕下雨，夏天不怕熱，冬天不怕冷，每天不停地幹。

有個老人叫智叟 (Zhìsǒu the Wise Old Man) ，看見愚公一家人在搬山，覺得很可笑，就對愚公説：“你這麼大歲數了，路也走不動了，能搬得動山嗎？”

愚公回答説：“你還沒有小孩子聰明！我雖然快要死了，但是我還有兒子，兒子死了，還有孫子。山上的石頭搬走一點兒就少一點兒。我們每天不停地搬，為什麼搬不走山呢？”

智叟聽了，沒有話説了。

四、注釋　Notes

1.　"天安門照得上照不上？"

"Can this photo include Tiananmen?"

2.　"啊，小朋友，謝謝你。"

"小朋友"is a affectionate form of address for children, e.g. "小朋友，去天安門怎麼走？"

3.　"我剛走開，就找不到你們了。"

The verb "開" may serve as a resultative complement, indicating movement away from a place, as in "跑開", "拿開椅子". It may also indicate separation of parts originally linked together, as in "開開門", "打開書".

4.　"這個廣場站得下一百萬人。"

The Naming of numbers above one thousand:

```
九百 ……………………九百九十九　一千
一千零一……一千零十九……一千一百
一千二百二十……一千八百零一…兩千
三千六百四十四…九千八百九十…一萬
一萬零一……九萬九千八百零三…十萬
十萬零一……八十二萬五千一百七十九
………………………………一百萬
```

Note that 1,000 is "一千" instead of "十百", and 10,000 is "一萬" instead of "十千". The character "萬" is used as the unit in naming numbers bigger than 10,000, as in "十萬、一百萬、一千萬" etc.

5.　"您對建築藝術很有研究啊！"

"對…很有研究" is used to describe someone is expert in a special field of knowledge.

(292,293,294)

6. "這麼大的建築，那時候只用了十個月就完成了。"

The demonstrative pronoun "這麼" (read as zème in colloquial speech) is often used to modify a verb or an adjective, denoting special quality, state, manner or degree, e.g. "這個漢字應該這麼寫。""天氣這麼冷，我不想出去了。"

五、替換與擴展 Substitution and Extension

(一)

1. 紀念碑上的字你看得見嗎？
   我看得見。

公園門口的石獅子，	看，	清楚
山上的亭子，	看，	見
操場上的廣播，	聽，	見
英文小說，	看，	懂
我說的話，	聽，	清楚
這個故事，	聽，	懂

2. 那些照片你明天洗得好洗不好？
   我想可以洗得好。

練習，	作，	完
生詞，	記，	住
事兒，	辦，	完
自行車，	修，	好
語法，	講，	完
書，	帶，	來

3. 他們找得到古波嗎?
   他們找不到。

買，	《李自成》
請，	顧問
聽，	這種音樂
吃，	中國菜
看，	京劇

4. 這個禮堂坐得下多少人?
   坐得下一萬人。

公共汽車（輛），	坐，	人，	45
房間（個），	放，	桌子，	2
廣場（個），	停，	車，	110
操場（個），	站，	人，	12,000
樓（個），	住，	家，	90

5. 這些活兒你一個人幹得了嗎?
   我幹不了。

衣服，	洗
工作，	完成
東西，	拿
圖片，	帶
冰棍兒，	吃
錢，	花

6. 行李這麼大，你拿得動嗎？
   可以，我拿得動。

```
自行車，舊，騎
東西，  多，拿
桌子，  重，搬*
```

7. 人民大會堂有多高？
   人民大會堂有四十六米高。

```
這張桌子，長，    100 公分
他哥哥，   高，    1 米 79
這種布，   寬，    2 尺*
這間臥室， 大，   18 平方米*
你的箱子，重，    15 公斤*
```

(二)

1. Making a telephone call

   A：喂，是小張嗎？我是小王。明天的球賽我參加不了
   了。

   B：你說什麼？請你說得慢點兒，我聽不清楚。

   A：我身體不太好，明天來不了。

   B：是嗎？太遺憾 (yíhàn pity; sorry) 了。你要多休息。

   A：謝謝你。對了，吃飯的時候你見得到古波嗎？

   B：有什麼事兒？

   A：請你告訴他一下兒，他要的書現在買不到。

B：好，我一定告訴他。

2. Inviting someone to an outing

A：星期天我們幾個人要騎車去景山公園。你想去嗎？

B：我很想去，可是我怕去不了。

A：為什麼？

B：星期天下午一點，有個朋友要來看我。十二點以前回得來嗎？

A：我想回得來。這麼好的天氣，你還是跟我們一起去吧？

B：好吧。

3. Describing a building

A：人民大會堂的大禮堂坐得下多少人？

B：坐得下一萬人。

A：有這麼大嗎？

B：大禮堂有七十多米寬，六十米長，三十三米高。大禮堂的主席台就坐得下五百人。

A：從電視裏看，大禮堂有三層，是嗎？

B：是啊！第一層坐得下三千六百多人，中間那層坐得下三千四百多人，最上邊那層也能坐二千四百多人。這三層和主席台一共有一萬多個座位，所以叫"萬人大禮堂"。

A：這麼大的禮堂，坐在後邊聽得清楚嗎？

B：聽得清楚。你有機會可以進去試一試。

六、語法　Grammar

1. The potential complement

A potential complement is formed with the structural particle "得" inserted between a verb and a resultative (or directional) complement. "聽得懂", "作得完" or "回得來" means the same as "能聽懂", "能作完" or "能回來". The negative of the potential complement is formed by replacing "得" with "不", as in "聽不懂", "作不完", "回不來". Here are some more examples:

今天的練習不多，晚上我作得完。

電話已經修好了，現在聽得清楚了。

他剛進城，吃飯以前回不來。

When a verb has an object, the object is placed after the potential complement. If the object is long and complicated, it is normally placed at the beginning of the sentence, e.g.

現在我還看不懂中文雜誌。

寄到上海的航空信明天收得到嗎?

The affirmative-negative interrogative form of a sentence with a potential complement is made by juxtaposing the affirmative and the negative forms of the potential complement.

你看得見看不見山上的亭子?

長城最高的地方你上得去上不去?

Points to be noted:

(1) The optative verbs "能" and "可以" also indicate possibility, but

(302,303,304)

in spoken Chinese, especially in sentences with resultative or directional complements, potential complements are preferred.

For emphasis a potential complement may sometimes be used together with an optative verb, e.g.

這輛自行車你自己能修得好嗎?

星期三以前我可以看得完這本小説。

However, when asking for permission, only optative verbs, instead of potential complements are used. For "May I come in?" the correct form is "我可以進來嗎？" but not "我進得來嗎？"

(2) The potential complement is the same in form with the affirmative of complements of degree – both have "得" inserted between the verb and the complement. They may be differentiated from the context and also in the following two ways:

① Unlike a potential complement, a complement of degree is often preceded by an adverbial modifier.

② Unlike a complement of degree, a potential complement is often followed by an object.

2. "下", "了" or "動" used as a potential complement

As a potential complement, "下" usually indicates there is enough room for a certain purpose, e.g.

這個櫃檯很大，放得下這麼多東西。

汽車裏擠不下八個人。

The verb "了(pronounced as liǎo)" is seldom used as a resultative complement or as a predicate by itself. But it is often used as a potential complement indicating possibility of an action. E.g.

我看明天要下雨，頤和園還去得了嗎?

老師病了，明天上不了課。

"了" sometimes has the same meaning as "完", e.g.

你喝得了這麼多茅台酒嗎?

我作這些練習用不了兩個小時。

The verb "動", when used as a potential complement, indicates capability of doing something. The foregoing verb usually denotes an action that causes changes of the position of a person or thing, e.g.

快到終點的時候，他已經跑不動了。

你不用幫我了，我自己拿得動這些東西。

七、練習　Exercises

1. Read aloud the following phrases:

作得完	看得見	聽得懂	找不到	回不來
出不去	記得住	買得到	見得到	聽不清楚
進不來	上不去	幹得了	拿得了	走得了
去得了	實現得了	完成得了	用不了	吃不了
修不了	回答不了	參加不了	修建不了	站得下
坐得下	放得下	掛不下	住不下	寫不下
拿得動　走得動	跑得動	騎不動	游不動	跳不動

2. Fill in the blanks with proper potential complements:

(1) 圖片上的字，你看 ＿＿＿＿＿＿ 嗎?

字太小，我看 ＿＿＿＿＿ 。

(2) 這麼大的行李你一個人拿 ＿＿＿＿＿ 嗎?

這件行李雖然大，但是不太重，我一個人拿 ＿＿＿＿＿ 。

(3) 這間房子住 ＿＿＿＿＿ 四個人嗎?

這間房子很大，住 ＿＿＿＿＿ 四個人。

(4) 我們明天去訪問一位退休老工人，你去 ＿＿＿＿＿ 嗎?

明天我沒空兒，去 ＿＿＿＿＿ 。

(5) 這本小說你買 ＿＿＿＿＿ 嗎?

這本小說書店裏沒有，現在買 ＿＿＿＿＿ 。

(6) 他住的地方你找 ＿＿＿＿＿ 嗎?

我有他的地址，一定找 ＿＿＿＿＿ 。

(7) 這個活兒很重，你們幾個人幹 ＿＿＿＿＿ 嗎?

你放心，我們幹 ＿＿＿＿＿ 。

(8) 外邊還在下雨，你們出 ＿＿＿＿＿ 嗎?

雨太大，我們出 ＿＿＿＿＿ 了。

3. Turn the following into the affirmative-negative questions with potential complements, then answer them:

Example: 今天的練習你能作完嗎?

（這些練習不太難）

→今天的練習你作得完作不完?

這些練習不太難，我作得完。

(1) 老師用中文講語法，你能聽懂嗎?

（他講得很慢，也很清楚）

(2) 學校的禮堂能坐下兩千人嗎?

（這個禮堂很大）

(3) 今天上午能見到那位顧問嗎?

　　（上午他去檢查工作了）

(4) 你們學院修建的新樓今年能完成嗎?

　　（工人們都在努力幹）

(5) 我們不坐車了，你能走去嗎?

　　（路不太遠）

(6) 這個照相機的鏡頭能修好嗎?

　　（沒問題）

(7) 這首古詩的意思你能看懂嗎?

　　（這首古詩生詞很多）

(8) 他們的問題你現在能回答嗎?

　　（我要想一想）

4. Describe the picture, using a potential complement where one is needed, then read the passage:

　　有一位老大娘正在公共汽車站等車。老大娘眼睛不太好，看不見字兒，她問我："同志，這車到火車站嗎?"

　　"到得了！"我說。

　　"這麽多人等車，這輛車坐得下嗎?"

　　"這輛車很大，坐得下這些人。"我問她："大娘，您

　　　　　　　　　　(309,310)

去哪兒？帶著這麼多東西，拿得了嗎？"

　　她説："這些東西不重，我拿得了。我現在身體還好，還走得動，就想到孩子那兒去看看。"

　　"您這樣上不去車，我幫您拿點兒吧！"

　　"謝謝！"

5. Read the dialogue, then write out the figures in Chinese characters:

　　A：這個大學有多少學生？

　　B：去年有 7,562 個學生，今年有 8,050 個學生。

　　A：解放以前這兒有幾千個學生？

　　B：沒有幾千，只有 1,100 個學生。

　　A：以後這個學校還要發展吧？

　　B：是啊！明年要有 10,000 個學生。

7,562 _____	個學生
8,050 _____	個學生
1,100 _____	個學生
10,000 _____	個學生

6. Translate the following into Chinese:

(1) This city has a history of over three thousand years. （千）

(2) How wide is the road? They say that it is 100 metres at the widest. （寬）

(3) As the door can't be opened, we are all waiting outside the auditorium. （…開）

(4) This is typical classical Chinese music. （典型）

(5) Why do you specialize in linguistics since you are so fond of art? （這麼）

(6) I'll go and see him some other time, as he is so busy today. （這麼）

7. Describe the following pictures in writing:

媽媽：看不見了！   大夫：看得見嗎？

小孩：看得見。   小孩：看不見了！

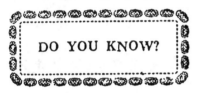

DO YOU KNOW?

(312,314,315)

第四十三課

一、課　文

快 坐 下 來 吧

帕蘭卡：古波，咱們從天安門走到這兒，我又累又餓，真走不動了。

古　波：是啊，咱們還沒有吃飯呢，我也有點兒餓了。咱們找個飯館吧，你看，那個女同志走過來了，我去問問。（問女同志）同志，請問這兒有飯館嗎？

女同志：有好幾家，可是吃飯的時間已經過了。你們往前走，看見大馬路，穿過去，那兒有一家北京風味的小吃店。

古　波：謝謝您。（對帕蘭卡）我早就聽說過北京的小吃不錯，咱們走吧。

　　　　　＊　　　　　＊　　　　　＊

（在小吃店）

古　波：你不是累了嗎？別站著了，快坐下來吧。

帕蘭卡：我看牆上的畫兒呢。那兒寫著"顧客之家"，是什麼意思？

古　波：顧客走進店裡來，就像走進自己的家一樣。是不是這個意思？

帕蘭卡：對。寫得真親切！

服務員：二位吃點兒什麼？那個牌子上寫著各種小吃，請先看看，我一會兒就來。

古　波：這麼多種，咱們吃什麼呢？

帕蘭卡：我餓了，多買點兒吧。

服務員：二位看好了嗎？

古　波：要兩碗元宵，兩碗豌豆粥，四個炸糕，四個油餅。

服務員：您要帶回去嗎？

古　波：不帶回去，就在這兒吃。我們沒有來過小吃店，請給我們介紹介紹。

服務員：您要得太多了，兩個人吃不了。我看這樣吧，先嘗嘗豌豆粥。北京人都知道"豌豆趙"——趙師傅作的豌豆粥最有名，他以前就在我們店裡。這兒的油餅也比較好，來四個油餅、兩個炸糕。要是不夠，再喝一碗杏仁豆腐，怎麼樣？

帕蘭卡：杏仁豆腐是什麼？

服務員：杏仁豆腐是用杏仁、牛奶、糖和別的東西作的，像豆

　　(317,318,319)

腐一樣，非常好吃。

古　波：好，就要這些。

服務員：一會兒給您送過來。

帕蘭卡：謝謝您的介紹，你們服務得真週到。

服務員：這是應該的。顧客走進來都希望吃得又好、花錢又少。我們作得還不夠，請您多提意見。

二、生　詞

1. 累	lèi	to feel tired
2. 餓	è	to be hungry; hungry
3. 有(一)點兒	yǒu (yì) diǎnr	a bit
4. 飯館	fànguǎn	restaurant
5. 穿(馬路)	chuān (mǎlù)	to cross (a street)
6. 風味	fēngwèi	local flavour; local style
7. 小吃店	xiǎochīdiàn	snack bar
小吃	xiǎochī	snack; refreshments
店	diàn	shop; store
8. 顧客	gùkè	customer
9. 之	zhī	a modal particle; a pronoun
10. 親切	qīnqiè	cordial; kind
11. 各	gè	each; every; various; respectively

12.元宵	yuánxiāo	sweet dumplings made of glutinous rice flour
13.豌豆粥	wāndòuzhōu	pea gruel
粥	zhōu	gruel; porridge
14.師傅	shīfu	master chef
15.炸糕	zhágāo	fried cake
16.油餅	yóubǐng	deep-fried pancake
17.比較	bǐjiào	comparatively; quite; to compare
18.夠	gòu	enough; sufficient
19.杏仁豆腐	xìngréndòufu	almond curd
杏仁	xìngrén	almond
豆腐	dòufu	bean curd
20.牛奶	niúnǎi	milk
21.糖	táng	sugar
22.別的	biéde	other; another
23.好吃	hǎochī	delicious; tasty
24.服務	fúwù	to serve
25.提	tí	to suggest; to put forward
26.意見	yìjiàn	criticism; comments or suggestions

專　名

豌豆趙	Wāndòu Zhào	name of a person

補　充　詞

1. 渴　　　　kě　　　　　　thirsty
2. 菜單　　　càidān　　　　menu
3. 綠燈　　　lǜdēng　　　　green light
4. 亮　　　　liàng　　　　　light; bright
5. 當心　　　dāngxīn　　　　to take care; to look out
6. 存車處　　cúnchēchù　　　parking lot (for bicycles)
7. 推　　　　tuī　　　　　　to push

三、閱讀短文

請　客

　　說話也是一種藝術。有的人說出話來讓人高興，有的人說出話來真氣人。我有一個朋友，他就不會說話。他一說話，聽的人就很不愉快。

　　有一次，他在飯館裡請客 (qǐng kè to invite someone to dinner)。那天他一共請了四位客人，來了三位，有一位還沒有來。他等得有點著急了，就說：" 你看，該來的沒來！" 坐在他旁邊的一位客人聽了以後，就覺得不高興。他想：" 該來的沒來——我是不該來的了？" 這位客人站起來說：" 對不起，我出去有點事兒。" 他走出餐廳去，對門口的服務員說：" 你告訴他們，不要等我了。"

過了一會兒，服務員走進來問："先生，您要的菜都準備好了，現在拿上來嗎？"

"別忙，我們在等人呢。"我朋友一看，少了一位客人，就問："那位去哪兒了？"服務員說："那位先生已經走了。"我朋友一聽，更著急了，就說："不該走的走了！"

這時候還有兩位客人坐在那兒等著。有一位聽了我朋友的話，心裡很不高興，他想："不該走的走了，意思是該走的還沒走，好，我是該走的，我現在就走！"他站起來，沒有說一句話就離開了飯館。

只有一位客人坐在那兒了。我朋友還在問自己："他們怎麼都走了？"這位客人說："您不是說該來的沒來，不該走的走了嗎？他兩位覺得自己是不該在這兒的了，所以他們都走了。以後您說話要注意點兒。"

"是啊，以後我一定要注意。"我朋友說，"可是，我說的不是他們啊！""什麼？"客人大聲地問："你說的是我啊？"這位客人也走了。

四、注釋　Notes

1. "我也有點兒餓了"

"有（一）點兒", meaning "a bit", is often used adverbially before certain adjectives and verbs to indicate a slight degree of something. When used before adjectives, the expression often suggests a slight degree of dissatisfaction. E.g. "有點兒累", "有點兒不高興", "有點兒像".

2. "有好幾家，可是吃飯的時間已經過了。"

"There are several restaurants here, but it is already past meal time."

When used before a measure word or a noun, "好幾" means "several", as in "好幾個" and "好幾天".

3. "那兒有一家北京風味的小吃店。"

"There is a snack bar serving food of Beijing style."

"小吃店", a snack bar or a buffet, supplies glutinous rice cakes, baked wheaten cakes, fried dough sticks, ravioli soup, etc. Food of this kind is also called "小吃".

4. "二位吃點兒什麼?"

"What would you like to have?"

5. "我看這樣吧，先嘗嘗豌豆粥。"

"I would rather suggest having a taste of the pea porridge first."

6. "來四個油餅、兩個炸糕。"

"來" is often used colloquially by customers, saleclerks or waiters to mean "buy" or "want", as in "來一瓶葡萄酒", "來一件襯衫吧".

7. "要是不夠，再喝一碗杏仁豆腐，怎麼樣?"

"怎麼樣" here has the same meaning as "好嗎", used for making suggestions or consulting others.

8. "杏仁豆腐是用杏仁、牛奶、糖和別的東西作的。"

"Almond junket is made from almond, milk, sugar and other ingredients."

五、替換與擴展 Substitution and Extension

(一)

1. 誰從前邊走過來了？
   他師傅從前邊走過來了。

裏邊，	出來
樓上，	下來
樓下，	上來
外邊，	進來

2. 那個顧客在哪兒呢？
   他走進飯館去了。

服務員，	走出，	小吃店
觀眾，	跑下，	樓
作家，	走上，	主席台
司機，	走回，	家
運動員，	游過，	河

3. 你從郵局拿回那封信來了嗎？
   我沒有從郵局拿回那封信來。

牆上，	拿下，	那張畫
香山，	帶回，	紅葉
樓下，	拿上，	兩瓶牛奶
外邊，	買回，	糖
老師那兒，	拿回，	本子

4. 他從小吃店買回來什麼了?

他從小吃店買回來四個油餅。

櫃檯裏,	拿出來,	兩碗杏仁豆腐
家裏,	帶出來,	一個照相機
那兒,	送過來,	兩個炸糕
樓上,	拿下來,	四個碗
箱子裏,	找出來,	兩件襯衫
學校裏,	帶回去,	一張獎狀

5. 你不是累了嗎? 怎麼不坐下來呢?

病,	休息休息
餓,	多吃一點兒
看完那本書,	還回去
寫好信,	寄出去
有意見,	給他們提

6. 他又累又餓。

高,	大
熱,	渴*
著急,	難過
親切,	週到
喜歡音樂,	喜歡文學
學語言,	學歷史

(二)

1. Dining in a restaurant

服務員：二位請到樓上去，那兒有兩個座兒。

顧客A：快坐下來吧，你今天累了。

師傅，有菜單＊嗎?

服務員：有，我給您拿過來。

顧客A：你想吃什麼?

顧客B：先來兩瓶橘子水吧，我渴＊極了。

顧客A：好。咱們要一個香酥鷄 (xiāngsūjī crisp chicken)，一個糖醋魚 (tángcùyú sweet and sour fish)，一個炒油菜 (chǎoyóucài stir-fried rape)，怎麼樣?

服務員：還要別的嗎?

顧客B：你愛吃豆腐，再來一個砂鍋豆腐 (shāguōdòufu bean-curd soup in earthen-ware pot) 吧。師傅，要等多長時間? 能不能快點兒?

服務員：要不了很長時間，一會兒就給 您送上來。

2. Going somewhere by bicycle

A：今天是星期六，馬路上車又多、人又擠，咱們從小路騎過去吧。

B：好。前邊是路口 (lùkǒu junction of streets)，騎慢一點兒。

A：綠燈＊亮＊了，快穿過去。

B：當心 (dāngxīn look out)！左邊汽車開過來了。

＊   ＊   ＊

A：同志，請下車。自行車不能騎進來。

B：對不起。我進去找一個人，車放在這兒，可以嗎?

A：存車處＊在那邊，請您推＊過去吧。

六、語法 Grammar

1. The complex directional complement

When followed by the simple directional complement "來" or "去", the verb "上", "下..", "進", "出", "回", "過" or "起" may function as complement to other verbs indicating direction of movement. Complements of this type are called "complex directional complements", as in:

他從外邊走進來了。

他從屋裏走出去了。

Following are some commonly-used complex directional complements:

	上	下	進	出	回	過	起
來	上來	下來	進來	出來	回來	過來	起來
去	上去	下去	進去	出去	回去	過去	

And they mean:

上來	– to come up		上去	– to go up
下來	– to come down		下去	– to go down
進來	– to come in		進去	– to go in
出來	– to come out		出去	– to go out
過來	– to come over		過去	– to go over

As in simple directional complements, "來" indicates movement towards the speaker or the object referred to, and "去" indicates movement away from the speaker or the object referred to.

When a sentence with a complex directional complement contains an object expressed by a noun of locality, the object should be placed before "來" or "去", e.g.

他跑上樓去了。

汽車不能開進公園裏來。

If the object is expressed by a word other than a noun of locality, it may be placed either before or after "來" or "去", e.g.

帕蘭卡每星期寄回一封信去。

帕蘭卡每星期寄回去一封信。

Generally "了" occurs at the end of this type of sentence, but it may also come after the verb if the verb has no object after it, e.g.

他給你帶回來那本小說了。

電車已經穿過廣場去了。

那個牌子已經拿下來了。

到了那個公園，嚮導先走了進去。

(332,333)

2. The construction "不是…嗎"

"不是…嗎" is often used to form a rhetorical question to indicate that what is said is true. It is usually employed to give emphasis to a statement, e.g.

他不是很努力嗎？ 為什麼學得沒有別的同學好呢?(他很努力

你不是很想看這個電影嗎？ 為什麼不去呢?(你很想看這個電影

"不…嗎" is used in a sentence with "是", e.g.

這不是你的錶嗎? (這是你的錶)

3. The construction " 又…又…"

The adverb " 又" may be used to indicate the simultaneous existence of various different circumstances or qualities.

" 又…又…" is used to link two coordinate verbs, adjectives, verbal structures or adjectival structures, indicating that the simultaneous existence of two circumstances or qualities, e.g.

女兒要走了，她心裏又高興， 又難過。

今天又颳風，又下雨。

他洗照片洗得又快又好。

七、練習 Exercises

1. Read aloud the following phrases:

走上來	走下去	跑過來	跑過去	帶進來
帶進去	拿出來	拿出去	寄回來	寄回去
坐下來	坐下去	開過來	開過去	跑出來

跑出去　　　送回來　　　送回去　　　站起來　　　跳下去

有點兒難　　　有點兒緊　　　有點兒奇怪

有點兒著急　　　有點兒肥　　　有點兒擠

有點兒激動　　　有點兒不好意思

比較忙　　　比較辛苦　　　比較寬　　　比較重

比較清楚　　　比較典型　　　比較熱烈　　　比較容易

別的同學　　　別的時間　　　別的地方　　　別的東西

別的知識　　　別的意見　　　別的語言　　　別的專業

別的意思　　　別的手續　　　別的機會　　　別的情況

又冷又餓　　　又多又好　　　又長又瘦　　　又說又笑

又高興又難過　　　又聰明又漂亮

又唱歌又跳舞　　　又畫畫兒又寫字

2. Fill in the blanks with proper complex directional complements:

(1) 前邊的那位老大爺走 ＿＿＿＿ 了，我跑 ＿＿＿＿ 問他：“請問哪兒有飯館？”

(2) 我們走 ＿＿＿＿ 一看，小吃店裏的顧客真不少。

(3) 我們坐 ＿＿＿＿ 以後，一個年輕的服務員走 ＿＿＿＿ 問我們：“二位，想吃點兒什麼？”

(4) 我朋友站 ＿＿＿＿ 看牆上的畫兒。

(5) 我們看見幾個人從樓上走 ＿＿＿＿，就問服務員：“同志，樓上也有小吃嗎？”

(6) 一會兒一個老師傅給我們送 ＿＿＿＿ 兩個炸糕和兩碗豌豆粥。

(7) 這個小吃店的炸糕作得比較好，我想買一點兒帶 ＿＿＿＿，讓他們也嘗嘗。

(8) 我們從飯館裏走＿＿＿＿＿的時候，已經是晚上七點了。

(9) 我們慢慢兒地走＿＿＿＿學校＿＿＿＿吧！

3. Complete the following sentences using complex directional complements according to the speaker's position:

(1) 她站在樓上對我們説：“那是我的行李，請你們幫我拿＿＿＿＿＿吧！”

(2) 小張在宿舍裏告訴我：“剛才我看見古波從這兒走＿＿＿＿＿了。”

(3) 我朋友在宿舍裏對我説，他昨天從城裏買＿＿＿＿＿兩本好書。

(4) 我站在景山下邊看見古波從山上走＿＿＿＿＿了。

(5) 他在禮堂前邊看見小張走＿＿＿＿禮堂＿＿＿＿了。

(6) 你的照相機在我這兒，請你在樓下等一等，我跑＿＿＿＿＿樓＿＿＿＿給你拿＿＿＿＿＿。

(7) 售貨員從櫃檯裏拿＿＿＿＿＿一件藍中山裝＿＿＿＿給我試一試。

(8) 他們在北京買了一點兒瓷器，暑假帶＿＿＿＿＿國＿＿＿＿＿。

4. Make sentences with the following phrases and point out the speaker's position in each case:

Example: 跑上來

　　　→古波從樓下跑上來告訴我們：“今天下午有足球比賽。”（説話人在樓上）

(1) 走進去　(2) 跑出去　(3) 寄回去

(4) 開過來　(5) 穿過去　(6) 拿下來

5. Translate the following into Chinese:
   (1) Having worked for the whole day, he is now feeling a bit hungry. （有點兒）
   (2) It's rather cold today. Have you got enough on? （比較，夠）
   (3) Are there any other restaurants here? （別的）
   (4) He is good at both taking and printing pictures. （又…又…）
   (5) Several new roads have been built in our city this year. （好幾…）
   (6) Aren't Shanghai-style dishes delicious? （不是…嗎）
   (7) He attends to customers of all types equally well. （各種）
6. Write a short composition based on the following pictures, trying to use sentences with the complex directional complements where possible:

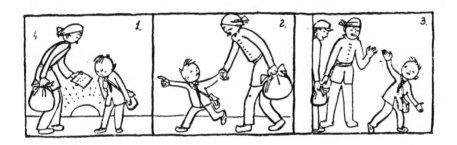

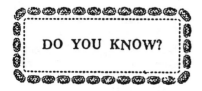

DO YOU KNOW?

Beijing Roast Duck

The Quanjude Restaurant is famous both at home and abroad for its roast duck it prepares. Quanjude, which literally means "a family of moral excellence", was opened in 1866.

Beijing roast duck, which can be traced back to over three hundred years ago, is prepared with specially raised Beijing crammed ducks using a particular and exclusive roasting process, and it has become one of China's traditional dishes of unique flavour. The Quanjude restaurant is noted especially for its "all-duck dinner", which means that all courses, hot or cold, are prepared from different parts of the duck. The restaurant serves 30 cold and 50 hot tasty dishes.

Outside Beijing's Hepingmen (Peace Gate), a new building has been erected recently for Quanjude in order to satisfy the needs of the customers both from home and abroad. It has a floor space of 15,000 square meters with 41 dining-halls and is capable of serving more than 2,500 customers simultaneously. The grandson of Mr. Yang Quanren, the founder of the Quanjude restaurant, is now on the managing committee of the restaurant.

(342,343)

第四十四課

一、課 文

她是跟貿易代表團來的

北京的十一月，天氣一天比一天冷了。古波和帕蘭卡決定星期天再到頤和園去一次。

他們走到頤和園門口的時候，後邊開過來一輛汽車。一個姑娘對著他們喊："帕蘭卡！古波！"帕蘭卡往車上一看，高興得跳起來："達尼亞，你是什麼時候到中國來的？"達尼亞從車上走下來說："我是十二號到的廣州，昨天剛從上海坐飛機到北京的。"

"你是來旅行的嗎？"

"不，我是跟貿易代表團來的。我們非常忙，只有星期天才有空兒。沒想到在這兒看見你們了，真是太好了。"

"你第一次到這兒吧？我們給你當嚮導，怎麼樣？"

他們一起走了進去。帕蘭卡先給這位老同學介紹了一下兒頤和園，她說："頤和園是中國有名的古典園林，它是一七五

　　　　　　　　(344,345)

○年開始修建的。第二年是皇帝母親的生日，所以這座山叫萬壽山。前邊的湖就是昆明湖。"

他們來到昆明湖邊。達尼亞激動地說："這兒又是水，又是山；湖上有橋，有小船；山上有古典建築，風景多麼美啊！"

帕蘭卡跟達尼亞到了長廊，她又介紹說："這就是有名的長廊。從東邊到西邊有七百二十八米，上邊畫了一萬四千多幅畫兒，有山水花草，也有人物故事。你看，那是古典小說《三國演義》裡的一個故事。"她們正在看畫兒，古波走過來說："上山去吧，那兒的畫兒更好看。"大家爬到山上一看，下邊的昆明湖像鏡子一樣。近的地方可以看到湖邊的亭子、綠樹；遠的地方可以看到藍天下的青山、白塔。這真是一幅又大又美的畫兒啊！

太陽下山了，他們才離開頤和園。

二、生　詞

1.	貿易	màoyì	trade
2.	決定	juédìng	to decide; to make up one's mind;
3.	喊	hǎn	to shout
4.	跳	tiào	to jump
5.	旅行	lǚxíng	to travel

6. 只有	zhǐyǒu	only
7. 園林	yuánlín	gardens; park; landscape garden
8. 它	tā	it
9. 母親	mǔqin	mother
10. 座	zuò	a measure word
11. 湖	hú	lake
12. 邊	biān	side; edge
13. 橋	qiáo	bridge
14. 船	chuán	boat
15. 風景	fēngjǐng	scenery; landscape
16. 多麼	duōme	how; what
17. 幅	fú	a measure word
18. 草	cǎo	grass
19. 人物	rénwù	figure; characters (in a play, novel, etc.)
20. 爬	pá	to climb
21. 鏡子	jìngzi	mirror
22. 近	jìn	near
23. 天	tiān	sky; heaven
24. 青	qīng	green
25. 塔	tǎ	pagoda
26. 太陽	tàiyang	the sun

專　名

1. 達尼亞　　　　Dániyà　　　　　　name of a person
2. 廣州　　　　　Guǎngzhōu　　　　name of a city
3. 萬壽山　　　　Wànshòu Shān　　　Longevity Hill
4. 昆明湖　　　　Kūnmíng Hú　　　　Kunming Lake
5. 長廊　　　　　Cháng Láng　　　　Long Corridor
6. 《三國演義》　《Sānguóyǎnyì》　name of a novel "Romance of the

　　　　　　　　　　　　　　　　　Three Kingdoms"

補　充　詞

1. 度假　　　　　dù jià　　　　　to spend one's holidays
2. 畢業　　　　　bìyè　　　　　　to graduate
3. 探親　　　　　tàn qīn　　　　to go home to visit one's family
4. 出差　　　　　chū chāi　　　　to be away on official business; be on

　　　　　　　　　　　　　　　a business trip

5. 生　　　　　　shēng　　　　　to be born
6. 對象　　　　　duìxiàng　　　　boy or girl friend
7. 生活　　　　　shēnghuó　　　　to live; life

三、閱讀短文

介 紹 對 象

"喂，小師傅，給你介紹一個對象*，怎麼樣？"星期六下午在回家的路上，售票員小王對我說。

"是誰？"我問她。

"一見面就知道了。明天上午十點在北海公園門口見……"話還沒說完，她就騎車走了。

小王是前年(qiánnián the year before last) 來我們這兒的。這一年多，我們常常在一起工作：我開車，她售票 (shòupiào to sell ticket) 。休息的時候，她還跟我學開車。她覺得我是汽車司機，參加工作的時間也比她長，總喜歡叫我"小師傅"。有一次我修車修到晚上十點多鐘，忘了吃晚飯，她就給我送來了熱飯熱菜。那是她自己在家裡給我作的。她比我小兩歲，可是對我的生活*很關心，真像我的姐姐。她自己還是一個沒有對象*的姑娘，現在要給我介紹對象*，多有意思啊！

星期天，我換了換衣服，九點多鐘就到公園門口去等她。一會兒，小王來了，她笑著問我："你是幾點來的？你來得真早。"

"我是騎車來的，九點半到的。"我心想，她是一個人來的，真奇怪，她要給我介紹的那個人在哪兒呢？

我們走進公園，她問我："你要找一個什麼樣 (shénmeyàng what kind of) 的人呢？"

我說："我想找一個在工作上和生活上都能互相幫助、互相關心的人。"

"你工作認真，學習努力，能幫助同志，也很關心大家，這些都是我應該學習的。可是，你今年已經二十五歲了，對自己的事兒怎麼不著急呢？"

我笑了笑，不知道應該怎麼回答。她看了看我，又說："會工作的人也應該會生活啊！"

我們在湖邊談了很多，談到了工作和學習，也談到了生活和理想*。我覺得她很了解我，我們談得非常高興，已經忘了時間。這時候，前邊走過來一個小朋友，問我："叔叔，幾點了？"我一看錶說："快十二點了！"

我站住問小王："我們談了這麼長時間，那個人一定等得很著急，她在哪兒呢？"

小王一點兒不著急。她笑了笑，臉一紅，不好意思地說："你啊，真是……"

這時候，我才注意到站在我面前的小王，今天穿得非常漂亮。我心裡一熱："啊！我真傻(shǎ stupid)……"

四、注釋 Notes

1. "北京的十一月，天氣一天比一天冷了。"

"It's November, and it's getting colder and colder in Beijing."

As an adverbial modifier, "一天比一天" indicates that changes increase or decrease progressively with the passage of time. A similar expression is "一年比一年", as in "他們的生活水平一年比一年高".

2. "帕蘭卡往車上一看，高興得跳起來。"

Here "跳起來" indicates the degree of Palanka's joy. Apart from adjectives, verbal structures may also be used as complements of degree, e.g. "她累得走不動了。".

3. "它是1750年開始修建的。"

"清漪園" (the Crystal Ripple Garden), built in 1750, was burnt down by the Anglo-French Allied Forces in 1860. The Empress Dowager Cixi had it rebuilt in 1888 with the navy funds and renamed "頤和園" (The Summer Palace).

4. "那是古典小說《三國演義》裏的一個故事。"

"Romance of the Three Kingdoms" is a well-known novel written by Luo Guanzhong, a novelist of the 14th century. The novel is based on historical facts and folklore. It describes the contradictions and struggles within China's feudal ruling class between 184 and 280 A. D.

五、替換與擴展 Substitution and Extension

(一)

1. 你母親到廣州去了沒有？

她到廣州去了。

她是什麼時候去的廣州？

她是上星期去的廣州。

> 天安門廣場，星期天上午
> 百貨大樓，　下午三點半
> 學校，　　　上午九點多
> 你弟弟那兒，昨天晚上

2. 他是從哪兒來的?
　他是從上海來的。
　他是跟誰一起來的?
　他是跟代表團一起來
　的。

> 城裏，他母親
> 工地，他師傅
> 飯館，他朋友
> 操場，教練
> 農村，他叔叔

3. 暑假你們去廣州了嗎?
　我們去了。
　你們是怎麼去的?
　我們是坐飛機去的。

> 故宮，走著
> 香山，坐公共汽車
> 上海，坐船
> 日本，坐飛機
> 景山公園，騎自行車

4. 他們是來工作的嗎?

　　他們不是來工作的，他們是來旅行的。

```
參觀，　　　服務
訪問，　　　談貿易
學習，　　　渡假*
學習建築，學習山水畫兒
研究音樂，研究園林
```

5. 後邊開過來一輛汽車。

```
前邊，　　走，人
那邊，　　跑，小孩
湖邊，　　走，老大爺
操場上，跑，外國學生
對面，　　穿，自行車
```

6. 這兒的風景多麼美啊!

```
湖，　　　大
塔，　　　高
橋，　　　長
天氣，　　熱
油餅，　　好吃
服務員，熱情
```

7. 你常常出來玩兒嗎?

不，只有星期天我才出來玩兒。

```
跳舞，            星期六晚上
爬山，            假日裏
坐公共汽車來，   天氣不好的時候
定作衣服，        買不到衣服的時候
```

(二)

1. Meeting of old friends

A：你不是張平嗎?

B：啊! 你是李國華。我們已經十多年沒有見了，對嗎?

A：是啊! 你是什麼時候離開南京的?

B：我是六四年離開的南京，你也是那一年畢業＊的吧?

A：不，我是六五年畢業＊的，那年秋天參加的工作。

B：那以後我們又見過一次，是不是?

A：對了，我是在北京看見你的。

＊   ＊   ＊

A：你是什麼時候到的北京? 怎麼不先寫封信來?

B：我也是三天以前剛決定的，已經沒有時間寫信了。

A：你這次是來探親＊的嗎?

B：不，我是來出差＊的，在這兒只住一個星期。

A：太短了! 明天你有空兒嗎? 到我家去玩兒，好嗎?

B：一定去。我是跟兩位同志一起來的，我要先告訴他
們一下兒。晚上我給你打個電話吧。

2. Talking about somebody's date and place of birth

A：你的孩子今年幾歲了？

B：十三歲了。

A：他是哪一年生＊的？

B：他是一九六八年生＊的。

A：他是在北京生＊的嗎？

B：不，是在上海生＊的。

3. Asking for criticisms

A：您聽了我們的介紹，也參觀了車間，現在請給我們
提提意見。

B：哪裏，我們是來學習的。今天的參觀對我們有很大
的幫助。

＊　　　　＊　　　　＊

六、語法　Grammar

1.　The construction "是…的"

"是…的" is used in a sentence to emphasize the time, place or manner of an action which took place in the past. "是" is placed before the word group that is emphasized ("是" may sometimes be omitted) and "的" always comes at the end of the sentence, e.g.

Noun or pronoun	"是"	Word(s) indicating time, place or manner	Verb	Noun or pronoun	"的"
客人	是	十點鐘	走		的。
他	是	從哪兒	買來	這些書	的?
你	是	寫信	告訴	他	的嗎?
我們	是	坐飛機	到	上海	的。

A verb-predicate sentence with "是…的" is different from an ordinary verb-predicate sentence stating that something happened in the past. In the first example sentence above, the emphasis is laid on "ten o'clock"—the time at which the guest left. If the sentence is changed into "昨天晚上十點客人走了", it would only be a simple statement of what happened yesterday.

If the verb in a "是…的" sentence has an object expressed by a noun, "的" may be put before the object, e.g.

　　　他是在房間裏找到的鉛筆。

　　　售票員問他："你是在哪兒上的車?"

If the object is a pronoun, or if the object is followed by a directional complement, "的" must be placed at the end of the sentence (see the table above).

The negative form of the sentence is "不是⋯的".

我們不是走來的，是騎自行車來的。

我不是一個人來的，我是跟朋友一起來的。

"是⋯的" may also be used to emphasize parts of a sentence indicating purpose, use or origin, e.g.

我是來問您問題的。

這張票是他買的。

這種錶是那個工廠生產的。

In sentence of this kind, "的" is always placed at the end.

2. The existential sentence

A verb-predicate sentence indicating the existence, appearance or disappearance of a thing or a person is called an existential sentence, e.g.

Phrase indicating locality	Verb	Particle or complement	Noun
窗口前邊	掛	著	一個牌子。
湖邊	坐	著	兩個年輕人。
樓下	來	了	一位客人。
從車裏	走	下來	幾個人。
廣場上	開	走了	幾輛車。

Sentences of this type always begin with a word of locality (or sometimes a word of time). The verb is generally followed by an aspect particle or a complement. The noun denoting a person or a thing is placed at the end (the noun is usually of indefinite reference, and it is wrong to say "前邊走來了他").

3. The construction "多麼…啊"

"多麼…啊" is used in exclamatory sentences expressing strong emotion. The adverb "多麼" (or the simplified form "多") always occurs before adjectives or certain types of verbs as an adverbial modifier. The sentence usually ends with the modal particle "啊", e.g.

那位服務員多麼熱情啊！

他的漢字寫得多漂亮啊！

我多麼喜歡中國的山水畫兒啊！

The structure "太…了", which has been discussed previously, is also used in exclamatory sentences, e.g.

太好了！

你騎得太快了！

4. The construction "只有…才…"

In the structure "只有…才…", the adverb "才" introduces circumstances that may appear only as a result of specific conditions, e.g.

只有多聽、多説、多唸才能學好一種外語。

只有到了秋天，才能看到香山的紅葉。

你只有自己去看一看，才能了解到那兒的情況。

"才" is often followed by "能，會，可以" or other optatives.

七、練習　Exercises

1. Read aloud the following phrases:

    是到上海去的　　是去北京的　　是來中國的

    是走着來的　　　是坐船去的　　是騎車來的

    是昨天去的　　　是秋天修建的　　是去年寄來的

    一天比一天熱　　一天比一天健康

    一天比一天高　　一年比一年多

    一年比一年發展　　一年比一年好看

    多麼激動啊　　　多麼重啊　　　多麼累啊

    多親切啊　　　　多近啊　　　　多週到啊

2. Answer the following questions using the words in the brackets:

    (1) 達尼亞是什麼時候去廣州的？

    　　她_____。（昨天晚上）

    (2) 他是怎麼去的天安門？

    　　他_____。（坐公共汽車）

    (3) 小王跟誰一起去頤和園的？

    　　她_____。（她母親）

    (4) 老華僑從美國坐飛機來的嗎？

    　　不，他_____。（從日本坐船）

    (5) 你的老同學是到中國來工作的嗎？

    　　不，他_____。（旅行）

    (6) 他為什麼來南京？

他 _____ 。（為幫助建設工廠）

3. Write a description of the picture (try to use sentences indicating existence, appearance or disappearance):

4. Translate the following into Chinese:

   (1) When was it that he decided to make a tour of China? （是…的）

   (2) How time elapses! （多麼…啊）

   (3) Only when one has mastered classical Chinese, is it possible for him to study classical Chinese poetry. （只有…才…）

   (4) If only it will be a sunny day tomorrow. （多麼…啊）

   (5) Watching the match, the spectators were so excited that they kept shouting. （激動得）

   (6) Spring has come. In parks trees are getting greener day by day. （一天比一天）

5. Read the following joke, then retell it:

   一個小女孩兒問她媽媽：“媽媽，爸爸是在什麼地方生*的？”

   “爸爸是在上海生的。”

"您也是在上海生的嗎？"

"不，我是在北京生的。"

"媽媽，我是在哪兒生的？"

"你是在廣州生的。"

"那麼 (nàme then)，我們三個人是怎麼認識的呢？"

6. Retell the story "介紹對象" in the third person.

第四十五課

復 習

一、課 文

看 熊 貓

中國的熊貓是非常珍貴的動物。以前在我們國家看不到，後來中國代表團送了兩隻去。我們的大動物園為這兩位客人修建了一個很漂亮的熊貓館。每天都有很多人去參觀。

我和古波來到北京以後，才知道中國人多麼喜歡熊貓啊！這兒的信封、本子、茶具、瓷器、鐘和小孩兒的衣服上常常畫著各種樣子的熊貓。我們還看過介紹熊貓的電影。

昨天，我和古波請張華光一起到北京動物園去看熊貓。北京動物園很大，裡邊有幾百種動物，不少是外國朋友送來的。小張指著正在吃草的大象說，它們有的是從南亞來的，有的是從非洲來的。

看了大象和獅子以後，我們來到熊貓館。裡邊人多極了，我們擠不進去。小張帶我們到了熊貓館的後邊，那兒有兩隻大熊貓正在吃竹葉。它們的樣子又可愛、又可笑：肥肥的身體，短短的腿，頭非常大，耳朵又這麼小，眼睛上像戴著墨鏡一樣。它們在竹子旁邊不停地走過來走過去。我覺得很奇怪：為什麼這兒人這麼少？一會兒從屋裡走出來一隻小熊貓。小朋友一看見它，就都跑了過來。有的還喊著："麗麗出來了！麗麗出來了！"小熊貓爬到它媽媽身上，看著給它們照相的人，就像在問："我這麼站，照得上嗎？"真可愛極了。

我問旁邊的一個小姑娘，"麗麗"是什麼意思？小姑娘告訴我，麗麗是這個小熊貓的名字。下星期麗麗就要坐飛機出國去了。我又問她："你以後就看不到麗麗了，你希望它留在這兒嗎？"

"希望。可是外國小朋友也希望早點兒看到麗麗啊！"小姑娘認真地回答。

我看著麗麗，心裡想：這些熊貓和大象不都是各國人民的友好"使者"嗎？

二、生　詞

1. 熊貓　　　　xióngmāo　　　panda

2. 珍貴　　　　zhēnguì　　　precious; valuable

3. 動物　　　　dòngwù　　　animal

4. 後來　　　　hòulái　　　afterwards; later

5. 隻	zhī	a measure word
6. 動物園	dòngwùyuán	zoo
7. 熊貓館	xióngmāoguǎn	panda exhibition hall
8. 樣子	yàngzi	manner; air; looks
9. 外國	wàiguó	foreign country
11. 它們	tāmen	they (refers to things, animals only)
12. 竹（子）	zhú(zi)	bamboo
13. 可愛	kě'ài	lovely
愛	ài	to love
14. 可笑	kěxiào	funny; ridiculous
15. 腿	tuǐ	leg
16. 頭	tóu	head
17. 戴	dài	to wear (e.g. cap, glasses, gloves)
18. 墨鏡	mòjìng	sunglasses
19. 使者	shǐzhě	emissary; envoy

專　名

1. 北京動物園	Běijīng Dòngwùyuán	the Beijing Zoo
2. 南亞	Nán Yà	South Asia
亞洲	Yàzhōu	Asia
3. 非洲	Fēizhōu	Africa
4. 麗麗	Lìlì	name of a panda

(373,374)

三、注釋 Notes

1. "後來，中國代表團送了兩隻去。"

"後來" can only be used to describe past events, while "以後" may be used for both past and future events. The sentence "以後我要更努力地學習" would be wrong if "以後" is replaced by "後來".

2. "我們擠不進去。"

"擠不進去" has the same meaning as "不能擠進去". A complex directional complement preceded by "得" or "不" may form a potential complement, as in "爬得上去", "帶不回來", etc.

3. "頭非常大，耳朵又這麼小。"

"又" (2), meaning "but" or "yet" here, is often used to connect two opposite ideas, e.g. "他剛才很高興，怎麼現在又哭了？" "我想去看足球，又怕下雨。"

四、看圖會話 Talk About These Pictures

1. Looking for somebody

…在嗎
…請進來
不進去了，…請…出來一下兒

2. Rendering a helping hand

到…去
拿得動
回得來

3. At a repair shop

修得好
修不好
看不清楚

4. At a hotel

是從哪兒來的
是什麼時候到的
是一個人來的

5. At a airport

走下來
開過去
走出去

6. Physical examination

有…高
有…重

五、語法小結 A Brief Summary of Grammar

1. Different kinds of complements
(1) The complement of degree
Complements of degree are generally formed of adjectives; verbal structures and adverbs may also function as complements of degree. Most complements of this type are followed by "得". A few, however, are not.

我們來得太晚了。

路上擠得開不了車。

從這兒到湖邊近得多。

這隻熊貓可愛極了。

(2) The resultative complement

他聽懂了嗎?

昨天他對我談到了這件事兒。

他還沒有決定住在北京。

小蘭的歌兒留住了兩位客人。

(3) The directional complement

古波著急,我們就先進來了。

別總是坐著了,快起來吧。

他還沒有回宿舍去。

今天的報一會兒給您送過來。

(377,378)

他雖然有點兒累，但是還要跟我們爬上那座山去。

最後三分鐘，我們隊踢進去一個球。

An object of locality cannot be placed at the end of a sentence that has a simple or complex directional complement.

(4) The potential complement

A potential complement is made up by "得" or "不" plus a resultative complement or a simple or a complex directional complement.

這個廣場站得下一百萬人。

她喝不了茅台酒。

這輛車上不去了，等下一輛吧。

這麼高你跳得過去嗎?

(5) The time-measure complement

他在上海住了三個多月。

他跑 100 米跑了 11 秒 2 。

我朋友學過兩年中國山水畫兒。

(6) The action-measure complement

他在電視裏看過幾次中國電影。

北京動物園他去過兩次。

他每天早上要打一遍太極拳。

(7) The complement of quantity

這件比那件大五公分。

這種墨鏡比那種貴兩塊多錢。

我的考試成績比他差一點兒。

2. The adverbs "就" and "才"
   "就"

(1) The adverb "就" indicates that the action referred to happened or will happen sooner, more quickly or smoothly than expected.

我們今年就能去。

他的孩子五歲就開始學畫畫兒了。

這個故事老師只唸了一遍，我們就聽懂了。

(2) It also indicates that the actions stated followed or will follow closely on each other.

我吃了午飯就去看足球賽了。

她買好了布就去定作衣服。

小蘭一看見我就說："照片上的阿姨來了。"

(3) "就" may be used to confirm what has been stated previously or to indicate what is said is true.

我就買這些明信片。

這就是有名的長廊。

(4) The adverb "就" indicate that the action referred to will soon happen.

(379,380)

飛機就要起飛了。

車就要拐彎了，請大家坐好。

請等一下兒，我一會兒就回來。

(5) "就" may also be used to refer back to the fact just stated and to indicate what may result form the fact.

走到山腳下，就能看見崇禎皇帝吊死的地方。

今天沒有課，我就不到學校去了。

就這麼辦，好嗎？

要是天氣好，就能看得更遠。

"才"

The adverb "才" is used to indicate:

(1) That the action referred to did or will not happen as soon, as quickly or smoothly as expected;

你怎麼現在才來？

我在路上走了一個多小時才到這兒。

他到書店去了三次才買到這本小說。

(2) That what is said will come true when certain conditions exist.

她只有星期天才有空兒出來玩兒。

我們來到北京以後，才知道中國人多麼喜歡熊貓啊！

你應該這樣練習，才能有更大的進步。

3. The structural particles "的" "得" and "地"

"的" is generally placed between an attributive modifier and the word that it modifies.

遠的地方可以看到藍天下的青山、白塔。

"得" is generally placed between a complement of degree (or a potential complement) and the predicate verb.

他們在這兒過得很愉快。

門太小，汽車開得進來嗎?

"地" is generally placed between an adverbial modifier and the predicate verb.

它們在竹子旁邊不停地走過來走過去。

六、練習 Exercises

1. Fill in each of the blanks with a character so as to form a word or a phrase with the character given:

園：__園，__園，__園，__園，園__

館：__館，__館，__館，__館，__館，__館

室：__室，__室

場：__場，__場，__場

堂：__堂，__堂，__堂

廳：__廳，__廳

房：__房，__房，房__，房__

Review the following groups of verbs, paying attention to their differences in meaning:

(1) 拿、帶、收、接、掛、放、指、換、交、幹、作

(2) 坐、站、跳、跑、走、穿、爬、進、出、起、睡

(3) 唸、說、講、談、喊、問、回答、介紹

(4) 想、喜歡、愛、感謝、忘、記、注意、放心、怕、決定

2. Turn the following verbs into the simple directional complements, and make sentences with them:

拿＿＿＿，送＿＿＿，過＿＿＿，帶＿＿＿，進＿＿＿，起＿＿＿＿

Turn the following into phrases with the potential complement, and make sentences with them:

Example:　走回來：走得回來　走不回來

　　　　→他從天安門走得回來。

跳過去：＿＿＿＿＿＿＿＿＿＿＿＿＿＿

拿上來：＿＿＿＿＿＿＿＿＿＿＿＿＿＿

開進來：＿＿＿＿＿＿＿＿＿＿＿＿＿＿

穿過去：＿＿＿＿＿＿＿＿＿＿＿＿＿＿

3. Expand the following sentences and turn the simple directional complements into complex directional complements:

Example:　老師下來了。

　　　　→我們的老師跟同學一起從樓上走下來了。

(1) 師傅回去了。

(2) 同學回來了。

(3) 熊貓過來了。

(4) 汽車過去了。

(5) 大象出來了。

(6) 司機下去了。

4. Fill in the following blanks with "就" or "才":

(1) 大家六點＿起床了，他七點半＿起。

(2) 他買了東西＿去看電影，所以他去晚了。

(3) 還有一個小時＿出發，現在還可以休息一下兒。

(4) 再過十分鐘火車＿進站了，快準備好。

(5) 明天下雨，我們＿不去動物園了。

(6) 今天的練習多極了，晚上不看電視＿能作完。

5. Translate the following into Chinese:

(1) Their children are very lovely. （可愛）

(2) He wants to visit the Zoo or the Summer Palace. He has not made up his mind yet. （又）

(3) It was three years ago that I left the village. Since then I have been working in this factory. （以後）

(4) He wants to learn how to paint, but doesn't want to spend time practising. That's why he is never learned to paint. （又）

(5) He is wearing a funny hat. （可笑）

(6) This precious photo was taken twenty years ago. （珍貴）

6. Mark the following sentences, using (+) for the correct ones and (−) for the incorrect ones:

(1) 他昨天又給我寄來了一封信。（　　）

(2) 我下午進了城去。（　　）

(3) 他們辛辛苦苦地工作了六個多月才寫完這本書。（　　）

(4) 我不能拿上去這張床。（　　）

(5) 他給你送一碗牛奶過來了。（　　）

(6) 這學期我學得完了第二本書。（　　）

(7) 你看得見看不見那兒的竹子？（　　）

(8) 明天他是坐火車來的。（　　）

(9) 樓上下來了古波。（　　）

(10) 我是在湖邊看見他的。（　　）

七、語音語調 Pronunciation and Intonation

1. Pause

Pauses are breaks made within a sentence or between sentences.

(1) Grammatical pause

Grammatical pauses are made on the basis of grammatical relationships between sentence elements. Pauses of this kind are very short (they are marked with the sign /). Grammatical pauses are usually made in the following places:

① A short pause is normally made after an attributive or an adverbial adjunct.

頤和園是中國有名的 / 古典園林。

達尼亞從車上 / 走下來。

② A pause is normally made also before a complicated object.

古波還看過 / 介紹熊貓的電影。

我沒有想到 / 在這兒看見你們了。

大家都說 / 香山的紅葉很好看。

③ A pause is usually made between the subject and the predicate.

二位 / 吃點兒什麼？

中國的熊貓 / 是非常珍貴的動物。

(2) Punctuation pause

Punctuation pauses are made according to punctuation marks. Pauses made at a full stop "。", an exclamation mark "！" or a question mark "？" are generally longer than pauses made at semi-colons "；", and pauses of the later kind are in turn longer than that made at commas "，". Pauses made at enumeration marks "　" are the shortest. Pauses made at colons "：", ellipses "……" and dashes "－" vary in length—sometimes longer, sometimes shorter. E.g.

A：你們看：／天安門、／華表、／石獅子都是典型的中
　　國古典建築。／我的話你們聽得懂嗎？

B：聽得懂。／老大爺，／天安門有多高？

A：有三十多米高。／天安門廣場／站得下一百萬人。

B：廣場真大啊！

A：廣場東邊是歷史博物館；／西邊是人民大會堂；／中
　　間是人民英雄紀念碑。／碑上邊有毛主席寫的字，／
　　你們看得見嗎？

B：看得見。

2. Exercises:

(1) Read aloud the following poem:

春天了。

又一個／春天。

黎明 (límíng daybreak) 了。

又一個／黎明。

呵，／我們共和國 (republic)的／萬丈 (zhàng a unit of length)

高樓／

　　　站起來了！

它，／加高了／
　　一層／
　　又／一層！

摘自賀敬之《放聲歌唱》

(2)　Read the following aloud:

　　"下雨天留客天留我不留"

　　這些漢字應該怎樣唸?

　　主人希望客人走，他是這樣唸的:

　　"下雨，／天留客。／天留，／我不留。"

　　客人看了這些字以後，他很高興。為什麼呢? 你看，他是這樣停頓的:"下雨天，／留客天。／留我不? ／留! "

第四十六課

一、課　文

她　把　藥　吃　了

丁大娘請帕蘭卡和古波星期日到她家去玩兒，但是星期六上午帕蘭卡病了。她頭疼、咳嗽，很不舒服。她想，昨天晚上她沒有把窗戶關上，可能感冒了。下午，她開始發燒，病得很厲害。古波把她送到了醫院。大夫說她是重感冒，要住院。

帕蘭卡住進了內科三〇二號病房。古波辦完住院手續走進病房的時候，她已經把藥吃了，正在床上躺著呢。她讓古波給丁大娘打個電話，告訴大娘明天他們去不了了。

星期日上午，古波又到病房來了。他手裡拿著一封信，一進門就說：“帕蘭卡，媽媽來信了。”帕蘭卡立刻坐起來說：“快給我！”古波把信給了她，又把桌子上的錄音機開開。帕蘭卡說：“你先把錄音機關上吧，等我看完信再開，好嗎？”

他們正說著話，聽見外邊有人敲門。古波開開門一看，是丁大娘和小蘭！丁大娘走到帕蘭卡的床前，關心地問：“姑娘，你哪兒不舒服？今天好點兒嗎？"帕蘭卡説："大娘，謝謝您，我好多了。昨天吃了藥，又打了針，今天量體溫，已經不發燒了。"丁大娘説："這我就放心了。昨天聽説你住院了，我真著急，小蘭也著急，一定讓我把她帶來。"

古波説："大娘，您快坐下！"

小蘭説："阿姨，嘗嘗我們家的葡萄。這是姥姥種的，我洗的。我把最大的給你帶來了。"

"謝謝你，小蘭真是好孩子。"

丁大娘説："帕蘭卡你想吃什麼？我給你作。"小蘭立刻跑過來，在帕蘭卡耳朵旁邊小聲地説："阿姨，您讓我姥姥包餃子。姥姥包的餃子好吃極了。"

"小蘭大聲説，要不，錄音機就錄不上了。"古波笑著説。

丁大娘問："你把我們説的話都錄上了？"

"都錄上了。我要給丁雲寄去，她聽到咱們的談話會多高興啊！"

一、生　詞

1. 把　　　　bǎ　　　　a preposition

2. 藥　　　　yào　　　　medicine

3. 疼　　　　téng　　　　ache; pain; sore

(395,396)

4.咳嗽	késou	to cough
5.舒服	shūfu	comfortable; well
6.窗户	chuānghu	window
7.關	guān	to close; to shut
8.可能	kěnéng	may; probable; possible
9.感冒	gǎnmào	to catch cold; (common) cold
10.發燒	fā shāo	to have a fever
11.厲害	lìhai	serious; terrible
12.醫院	yīyuàn	hospital
13.住院	zhù yuàn	to be in hospital; to be hospitalized
14.病房	bìngfáng	ward (of a hospital)
15.躺	tǎng	to lie
16.手	shǒu	hand
17.立刻	lìkè	immediately; at once
18.錄音機	lùyīnjī	(tape) recorder
19.錄音	lù yīn	to record; recording
20.打（針）	dǎ (zhēn)	to give or have an injection
21.針	zhēn	injection; needle
22.體溫	tǐwēn	(body) temperature
23.姥姥	lǎolao	(maternal) grandmother; grandma
24.種	zhòng	to grow; to plant

24. 小聲	xiǎoshēng	in a low voice; (speak) in whispers
25. 包	bāo	to wrap; to make (dumplings)
26. 餃子	jiǎozi	dumpling

補 充 詞

1. 病人	bìngrén	patient
2. 護士	hùshi	nurse
3. 掛號證	guàhàozhèng	register card
4. 科	kē	department (of internal medicine, etc.)
5. 大便	dàbiàn	stool; human excrement
6. 解	jiě	to relieve oneself
7. 藥方	yàofāng	prescription
8. 藥劑士	yàojìshì	druggist; pharmacist
9. 片	piàn	a measure word, tablets

三、閱讀短文

三 個 笨 人

　　古時候有一個縣官(xiànguān county magistrate) ，他覺得自己很聰明。一天，他對差役(chāiyì runner in a feudal yamen) 說："我給你們三天的時間，你們要在外邊找到三個笨 (bèn foolish)人，帶到我這兒來。"

第一天他們沒有找到。

第二天，他們看見一個人騎著馬，手裡還拿著一個很大的行李。他們走過去問他：“你騎在馬上，為什麼還自己拿著行李呢？”那個人說：“我騎在馬上，馬已經很累了，再放一個行李，不是更重了嗎？”差役一聽，高興極了：第一個笨人找到了。他們把他帶走了。

第三天他們走到城門口，看見一個人拿著竹子進城。城門很小，他的竹子又很長，他先豎著(shù zhe vertically) 拿，拿不進去；又橫著 (héng zhe horizontally) 拿，也拿不進去。他非常著急。後來把竹子折斷(zhé duàn to break up) 了，這才拿進去了。差役一看，第二個笨人又找到了。他們把他帶走了。

第四天，差役帶著這兩個人去見縣官。他們把這兩個笨人幹的事兒，告訴了縣官。縣官聽了，笑著對第二個笨人說：“你真笨極了！你怎麼不把竹子從牆上扔 (rēng to throw) 過去呢？”差役聽了，立刻說：“我們還找到了第三個笨人。”縣官往下邊看了看，奇怪地問：“這兒只有兩個人，第三個在哪兒？”差役說：“第三個笨人就是您！”

四、注釋 Notes

1. "她想，昨天晚上她沒有把窗戶關上，可能感冒了。"

As a resultative complement, "上" is often used to indicate that the completion of an action has brought about certain result such as coming together or being closed up. E.g. "關上門", "關上錄音機".

2. "大夫說她是重感冒。"

"The doctor said she'd caught the flu."

"他得了…", or "他是…" are usually used to state that someone has contracted a certain disease, e.g. "他得了感冒", "他是肺炎".

3. "古波把信給了她，又把桌子上的錄音機開開。"

The adverb "又" (3) sometimes has the meaning "in addition to", e.g. "昨天吃了藥，又打了針。"

4. "你哪兒不舒服？"

"What's troubling you?"

Two other expressions with similar meaning are "你怎麼不舒服？" and "你怎麼了？"

5. "我好多了。"

"I'm feeling much better."

In addition to "…得多", "…多了" may also be used to show that the difference between the two things referred to is great, e.g. "我比他大多了", "這種葡萄好吃多了".

6. "這我就放心了。"

"That makes me feel much easier."

7. "要不，錄音機就錄不上了。"

As a resultative complement, "上" denotes that something assumes a certain position or becomes attached to an object as a result of an action performed on it, e.g. "寫上他的名字", "戴上眼鏡".

五、替換與擴展 Substitution and Extension

㈠

1. 她把<u>藥</u><u>吃</u>了嗎?
   她把藥吃了。

牛奶,	喝
衣服,	洗
那本小說,	還
練習本子,	交

2. 請你把<u>錄音機</u><u>開開</u>,
   好嗎?
   好。

門,	開開
箱子,	開開
窗戶,	關上
電視,	關上

3. 你把<u>我們的話</u>都<u>錄上</u>了嗎?
   都錄上了。

花兒,	種上
衣服,	穿上
餃子,	包好
今天的練習,	作完
這些生詞,	記住

4. 他們想把什麼帶來?
   他們想把葡萄帶來。

寄來，	糖
拿來，	中國畫兒
送去，	獎狀
寄去，	綢子

5. 他把信給你了沒有?
   他還沒有把信給我。

這件事兒，	告訴
那張照片，	送
照相機，	還

6. 你把體溫量一量吧。
   我已經量過了。

心臟，	檢查檢查
血壓，	量一量
這個錄音，	聽一聽
身體情況，	談一談
要帶的東西，	檢查檢查

(二)

1. Registering (at a hospital)

   病人*：同志，我要掛號。

   護士：請把您的掛號證*給我。您看哪一科*?

   病人：內科。

   護士：內科在二樓。您到那兒去等著吧。

2. Seeing a doctor

   護士：25號，請進來。

大夫：你怎麼了？

病人：我發燒，頭疼得屬害，不想吃東西。

大夫：咳嗽嗎？

病人：有點兒。

大夫：你是什麼時候開始不舒服的？

病人：昨天下午我覺得有點兒發燒，晚上又開始頭疼。

大夫：大便＊正常嗎？

病人：正常。

大夫：把衣服解＊開，我聽一聽……好，請把衣服穿上
　　　吧。

病人：大夫，您說我是什麼病？

大夫：是感冒，沒有別的病。這是你的藥方＊。打幾針，
　　　吃點兒藥，休息兩天就好了。

3. At the pharmacy

病人：這是我的藥方，在這兒交錢嗎？

護士：不，你到旁邊的窗口交錢，再到對面拿藥。

　　　　　　……

病人：這些藥怎麼吃？

藥劑士＊：每天三次，每次大、小各兩片＊。

　　　　　明天上午還要來打一針。

＊　　　　　＊　　　　　＊

六、語法 Grammar

"把" sentences

"把" sentences are the most commonly-used type of verb-predicate sentence. They are generally used to emphasize how a person or thing is disposed of, and the result thereof. The performance of the action often causes the object to change position or to change from one state to another, generally affecting it in some specific way. For example, to the question "What did you do?" the answer may be "我洗衣服了". But to the question "What will you do with your dirty clothes?" or "Are your dirty clothes still there?" the answer may be "我把衣服洗了". Other possible answers related to the disposal of the clothes are "我把衣服穿上了", "我把衣服放在箱子裏了", etc.

In a "把" sentence, the preposition "把" and its object-the person or thing disposed of, are always put after the subject and before the verb. The whole prepositional structure functions as an adverbial modifier.

Noun or pronoun	Preposition "把"	Noun or pronoun (disposed of)	Verb	Other elements
我	把	這件事兒	忘	了。
（請）你	把	門	開	開。
你	把	錄音機	帶	來了嗎？
他	把	書	整理	得很好。
古波	把	信	給	她了。
你	把	學過的生詞	寫	一寫。

From the example sentences given above we can see:

(1) In a "把" sentence the main verb is normally a transitive verb having a sense of disposal or control. Verbs such as "有、在、是、來、去、回、喜歡、覺得、知道", etc. do not belong to this category, and cannot be used in "把" sentences.

(2) Generally speaking, the object of a "把" sentence is a definite person or thing in the mind of the speaker. Hence, instead of "我想把一本書看一遍", we should say "我想把那本書看一遍".

(3) To indicate how a person or thing has been disposed of or what has resulted from the disposal, the verb of a "把" sentence must be followed by other elements such as a complement (potential complements excepted), or an object. Otherwise the verb should be repeated. Hence instead of "他把錄音機開", we should say "他把錄音機開了", or "他把錄音機開開了".

Negative adverbs, optative verbs or adverbial modifiers of time, are normally placed before "把", e.g.

他還沒有把信寫完。

我們要把身體鍛鍊好。

他明天把照相機帶來。

The example sentences above can be turned into ordinary verbal-predicate sentences: "請你開開門", "古波給她信了", "我們要鍛鍊好身體", etc. These new sentences are general statements of fact, while the original "把" sentences are used in a strong sense of disposal of the objects related.

七、練習 Exercises

1. Read aloud the following phrases:

頭疼　脚疼　腿疼　手疼　有點兒疼

不舒服　睡得很舒服　房間很舒服

可能來　可能晚一點兒　有可能

沒有可能　很可能　不太可能

病得厲害　疼得厲害　熱得厲害

厲害的病　厲害的人　厲害的動物

2. Insert "把" into the sentences, making other necessary changes and use them as answers to the questions in the brackets:

Example:　我已經關上電視了。（你還在看電視嗎？"）

　　　　　→我已經把它關上了。

(1) 我開開窗戶了。（房間裏為什麼這麼冷？）

(2) 我已經看完這本小説了。（這本小説再讓你看三天，好嗎？）

(3) 她拿走了你的錄音機。（我的錄音機呢？）

(4) 小蘭已經洗好了葡萄。（你去洗一洗葡萄，好嗎？）

(5) 他已經送我這本雜誌了。（這是他的雜誌嗎？）

(6) 他已經告訴我這件事兒了。（這件事兒你還不知道吧？）

3. Make "把" sentences with the phrases given, paying attention to the elements after the verbs:

Example:　這本小説　翻譯

　　　　　→他把這本小説翻譯完了。

(1) 航空信　寄

(2) 這些東西　包

(3) 上一課的生詞　記

(4) 一百米的記錄　打破

(5) 那個故事　講

(6) 他朋友　送

4. Translate the following into Chinese:

(1) Can they complete the building this year? (把　修建)

(2) May I take this novel back with me? (把　帶)

(3) I assure you that I won't forget about the matter. (把　忘)

(4) He is not sure whether the doctor can cure him of his illness.
(把　看)

(5) Xiao Lan helped her granny and persuaded the guests to stay.
(把　留)

(6) It is getting cold. You'd better put on your cotton-padded jacket.
(把　穿)

(7) He has planted many flowers in the garden, and a number of trees
as well. (又)

(8) I have a headache today, and a cough too. (又)

(9) She felt much better after the injection. (…多了)

(10) We are much busier this term than last term. (…多了)

5. Answer the following questions on the text:

(1) 帕蘭卡和古波為什麼星期天不能到丁大娘家去了?

(2) 帕蘭卡哪兒不舒服?

(3) 她得了什麼病? 她是怎麼病的?

(4) 第二天古波給她帶來了什麼?

(5) 她為什麼不讓古波把錄音機開開?

(6) 丁大娘和小蘭為什麼也來了?

(7) 帕蘭卡身體好點兒了嗎?

(8) 小蘭對帕蘭卡說了些什麼?

(9) 古波為什麼要小蘭大聲說話?

(10) 古波為什麼要錄音?

6. Retell the story of the Reading Text with the help of the following pictures:

*   *   *

第四十七課

一、課　文

她把感想寫在留言簿上

　　昨天古波和帕蘭卡參觀了魯迅的故居。故居在北京阜城門外西三條二十一號。

　　講解員給他們介紹了故居的情況。他說，魯迅先生在一九二四年買了這套房子，他自己設計，把它修成現在的樣子。

　　他們走到院子裏，這兒的樹都是魯迅先生自己種的。古波一看到這些樹，就想到魯迅先生在一篇文章裡寫過："在我的後園，可以看見牆外有兩株樹，一株是棗樹，還有一株也是棗樹。"他問講解員："還有兩株棗樹嗎？"講解員說："有，一會兒我們到後園就看見了。"

　　講解員告訴他們："南房是魯迅的客廳，西房是厨房。北房三間，東邊是魯迅母親的臥室，西邊是書房，中間是餐廳。在北房後邊接出一間，北京人把這種房子叫作＇老虎尾巴＇，這就是魯迅先生的臥室，也是他寫文章的地方。"他們走進去

　　　　　　　　(416,417,418)

一看，房間很小。除了一張床以外，還有一張舊桌子和兩把椅子，真是儉樸極了。帕蘭卡看著這張舊桌子，心裡想：魯迅先生的《彷徨》、《野草》……就是在這兒寫的啊！

古波指著東牆上的一張照片問：“這是誰的照片？”講解員說：“這就是藤野先生。他們分別的時候，藤野先生把這張照片送給了魯迅。魯迅回到中國以後，非常懷念這位日本老師，把他的照片掛在自己的房間裡。你們讀過《藤野先生》這篇有名的文章吧？”

從老虎尾巴出來，他們來到了客廳。講解員說：“這兒常常有年輕的客人來訪問他。魯迅先生總是熱情地幫助他們，他培養了不少青年作家。進步青年都把魯迅先生看作自己的好老師、好朋友。”

參觀完故居，講解員把他們送到門口。古波對講解員說：“謝謝您的介紹。”帕蘭卡把自己的感想寫在留言簿上：“偉大的文學家魯迅，生活多麼儉樸，但是他給各國人民留下的文化遺產又是多麼豐富啊！”

二、生　詞

1.感想	gǎnxiǎng	impressions; feeling
2.留言簿	líuyánbù	visitors' book
留言	líu yán	to leave one's comments; to leave a message

3.故居	gùjū	former residence
4.講解員	jiǎngjiěyuán	guide
講解	jiǎngjiě	to explain
5.設計	shèjì	to design
6.成	chéng	to become; to turn into
7.院子	yuànzi	courtyard
8.篇	piān	a measure word
9.文章	wénzhāng	writings
10.棗樹	zǎoshù	jujube tree; date tree
11.株	zhū	a measure word
12.北邊	běibiān	north; northern part
13.間	jiān	a measure word
14.接	jiē	to extend; to connect
15.老虎	lǎohǔ	tiger
16.尾巴	wěiba	tail
17.除了⋯以外	chúle...yǐwài	besides; except
18.把	bǎ	a measure word
19.儉樸	jiǎnpǔ	simple and unadorned
20.懷念	huáiniàn	to cherish the memory of; to think of
21.培養	péiyǎng	to foster; to bring up
22.青年	qīngnián	youth

23.作	zuò	to regard as; to take (somebody) for
24.偉大	wěidà	great
25.文學家	wénxuéjiā	writer; man of letters
26.生活	shēnghuó	life; to live
活	huó	to live; alive; living
27.遺產	yíchǎn	heritage
28.豐富	fēngfù	rich; abundant; to enrich

專　名

1.阜城門	Fùchéngmén	name of a place in Beijing
2.西三條	Xīsāntiáo	name of a place in Beijing
3.《彷徨》	《Pánghuáng》	name of a collection of short stories
4.《野草》	《Yěcǎo》	name of a collection of prose poems
5.藤野	Téngyě	name of a person

補　充　詞

1.辦公室	bàngōngshì	office
2.錯誤	cuòwù	mistake
3.改	gǎi	to correct
4.出院	chū yuàn	to leave hospital
5.恢復	huīfù	to recover

6. 紀念	jìniàn	to commemorate; commemoration
7. 牛馬	niúmǎ	oxen and horses; beasts of burden
8. 群眾	qúnzhòng	mass; people

三、閱讀短文

有 的 人

——紀念魯迅有感

有的人活著
他已經死了；
有的人死了
他還活著。

有的人
騎在人民的頭上：" 啊，我多偉大！"
有的人
俯 (fǔ to bow) 下身子給人民當牛馬*。

…………

有的人
他活著別人就不能活；
有的人

他活著為了多數 (duōshù majority) 人更好地活。

騎在人民頭上的，

人民把他摔垮 (shuāi kuǎ to overthrow)；

給人民作牛馬的，

人民永遠記住他！

…………

他活著別人就不能活的人，

他的下場 (xiàchang end) 可以看到；

他活著為了多數人更好地活著的人，

群眾*把他抬舉(táijǔ highly praise) 得很高，很高。

（節選自＜臧克家詩選＞）

四、注釋 Notes

1. "古波一看到這些樹，就想到魯迅先生在一篇文章裏寫過…"

This is the essay entitled "Autumn Night", included in Lu Xun's collection of prose poems "Wild Grass".

2. "這就是藤野先生。"

Mr. Fujino Gamkulo (1874–1945), a native of Fukui County, Japan, was a teacher at the Sendai Medical School where Lu Xun studied between April of 1902 and the summer of 1906. Mr. Fujino gave him a lot of help. Lu Xun began his career as a writer in Tokyo after he left Sendai.

五、替換與擴展 Substitution and Extension

(一)

1. 她把自己的<u>感想</u>寫在哪兒了？

她把自己的感想寫在<u>留言簿上</u>了。

棗樹，種，	院子裏
鏡子，	掛，牆上
自行車，	放，門口
收信人的名字，寫，	上邊

2. 他們想把房子修建成那種樣子嗎？

　　對了，他們想把房子修建成那種樣子。

這篇文章，	翻譯，	英文
這個故事，	寫，	小說
這些青年，	培養，	運動員
禮堂，	設計，	中式的
新買的布，	作，	棉襖

3. 他們把這間臥室叫作什麼？

　　他們把這間臥室叫作"老虎尾巴"。

魯迅先生，	看，	自己的老師
張華光，	叫，	小張
丁師傅，	選，	車間主任
她，	看，	自己的女兒

4. 他把客人送到汽車站了嗎？

　　他沒有把客人送到汽車站。

他姥姥，	送，	醫院
錄音機，	拿，	病房
照片，	寄，	日本
汽車，	開，	院子裏
糖，	放，	牛奶裏

5. 請你把這張照片送給我，可以嗎？
　　可以。

這些葡萄，	帶，	我母親
這幅畫兒，	寄，	那位講解員
這件事兒，	交，	我們
《野草》，	還，	圖書館
麵包，	拿，	我

6. 除了《藤野先生》以外，你還看過什麼？
　　我還看過《藥》。

獅子和老虎，	看，	熊貓
歷史，	學，	藝術
竹子，	畫，	梅花
工廠，	參觀，	農村

7. 除了他們倆以外，別的人都沒有去魯迅的故居嗎？
　　除了他們倆以外，別的人都沒有去魯迅的故居。

帕蘭卡，	沒有得感冒
她們倆，	去旅行
你，	喜歡爬山
她，	會洗照片

1. Making an appointment

    A：老師，我有幾個問題想問您一下兒，您什麼時候有
    空兒?

    B：除了星期三以外，每天下午我都在辦公室＊。

    A：明天下午我去找您，可以嗎?

    B：你來吧。

    A：除了課文上的問題以外，練習本上我還有些不懂的
    地方。

    B：好，明天下午把你的練習本子帶來吧。

2. Coaching

    B：你知道這句話為什麼不對嗎?

    A：我把"以後"寫成了"後來"。

    B：除了這個詞以外，還有別的錯誤＊嗎?

    A：我想一想。對了，應該把"因為"放在"他"的前邊。

    B："因為"放在前邊跟放在後邊一樣。這句話應該改＊
    成這樣……

3. Visiting a patient

    A：小王，你覺得怎麼樣? 好點兒嗎?

    B：謝謝你，我今天好多了。

    A：你快躺下，別起來了。這是送給你的花兒。同學們讓
    我把錄音機帶給你。要是你覺得舒服點兒，可以聽聽
    音樂。

    B：謝謝大家的關心。請大家別來看我了，我很快就要出

院＊了。

A：別著急，再好好兒地休息幾天。希望你早點兒恢復＊
健康。

　　＊　　　　＊　　　　＊

六、語法　Grammar

1.　Some special types of "把" sentences

"把" sentences, rather than the ordinary types of verb-predicate sentences, should be used for the following situations:

"把" sentences should be used when the main verb is followed by the
resultative complement "在" or "到", and an object expressed by a noun of
locality, indicating the position that a person or thing occupies as a result
of an action performed on it, e.g.

你把棗兒放在哪兒了？

他把筆忘在家裏了。

我已經把那把椅子拿到樓上去了。

他們把我送到車站才跟我說"再見"。

"把" sentences should be used when the main verb is followed by the
resultative complement "成" or "作" and an object expressive of result,

－ 275 －

indicating what a person or thing disposed of by the action of the verb becomes. E.g.

他把"大夫"兩個字唸成了 dàfu。

他們用了三年的時間把這個車間發展成一個工廠。

他們都把她看作家裏人。

上海人把"喝茶"叫作"吃茶"。

"把" sentences are sometimes also used when the main verb is followed by the resultative complement "給" and an object, indicating that something has been handed over to a recipient as a result of an action performed, e.g.

我把錢交給了售票員。

他把我們介紹給文化參贊。

小張把這碗餃子留給古波嘗嘗。

2. The construction "除了⋯以外"

"除了⋯以外"（"以外" may be omitted), meaning "in addition to" or "besides" is often followed by adverbs such as "還", "也" or "又", e.g.

房間裏除了一張床以外，還有一張舊桌子和兩把椅子。

除了她以外，還有兩個同學也覺得不舒服。

昨天下午除了游泳，他還釣魚了。

這位護士除了工作認真，生活也很儉樸。

"除⋯以外" also means "except", often followed by adverbs such as "都" or "沒有", e.g.

(430,431,432)

除了他騎自行車去以外，我們都坐公共汽車去。

除了冬天冷一點兒以外，這兒的氣候很不錯。

除了棗樹，院子裏沒有別的樹了。

七、練習 Exercises

1. Read aloud the following phrases:

設計成　　培養成　　修建成　　排成　　換成

叫作　　看作　　選作　　留作　　唸作　　用作

培養青年　　培養學生　　培養作家

培養教練　　培養司機

偉大的國家　　偉大的人民　　偉大的文學家

偉大的藝術家　　偉大的建築

豐富的文化遺產　　豐富的知識

豐富的生活　　豐富的東西

2. Fill in the blanks with appropriate phrases:

(1) 講解員把參觀的人_____院子裏。

(2) 我已經把上個月買的綢子_____裙子了。

(3) 帕蘭卡在留言簿上寫完自己的感想以後，古波看了看，也
把自己的名字_____留言簿上了。

(4) 古波很喜歡這位青年作家的文章，他想把他_____英文。

(5) 他給小王一張法國地圖，小王把它_____宿舍的牆上。

(6) 飛機八點起飛，司機七點鐘開車把他們_____機場。

(7) 下午你看見她的時候，把這封信_____她，好嗎?

(8) 他把這次假期旅行 ＿＿＿＿了解中國的好機會。

3. Answer the following questions on the text:

(1) 魯迅先生把他買的房子修建成什麼樣子？

(2) 古波把講解員介紹的情況寫在本子上了沒有？

(3) 魯迅先生把那些樹種在什麼地方？

(4) 他把藤野先生的照片掛在哪兒？

(5) 魯迅的臥室裏放著一些什麼東西？

(6) 進步青年為什麼把魯迅看作自己的老師和朋友？

(7) 帕蘭卡在留言簿上寫了些什麼？

4. Make sentences with "把" and the words given:

(1) 梅花　　　種在

(2) 餃子　　　留給

(3) 紅葉　　　放在

(4) 孩子　　　培養成

(5) 汽車　　　停在

(6) 風景照片　　　寄到

5. Translate the following into Chinese:

(1) In addition to short stories, Lu Xun wrote a great many essays.
（除了…以外）

(2) What comments would you like to make on the essay that you have read?（感想）

(3) She likes all kinds of dishes except fish.（除了…以外）

(4) Young people now have much richer recreational activities than before.（豐富）

(5) Apart from this house, Lu Xun lived in three other places in Beijing.
（除了…以外）

(6) A great number of doctors have been trained for the country in this college. (培養)

6. Fill in the blanks with the verb "拉" (la to pull) or "推" (tui to push):

In the following picture, there are two railroad cars and a locomotive, which are stopped in positions A, B and C respectively. E is the location of a bridge, which is only wide enough for the locomotive to pass through. The driver is asked to use the locomotive to pull No.1 car into position B and No.2 car into position A. Then he has to move the locomotive back to its original position C. How will the driver manage to do this?

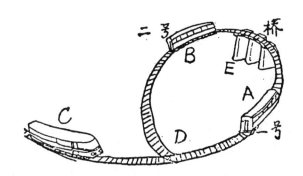

(1) 他先用火車頭 (huǒchētóu locomotive) 把二號從 B ＿ 出來，再 ＿ 到 C。

(2) 他把一號從 A ＿ 到 B。

(3) 他把二號從 C ＿ 到 A。

(4) 他把一號從 B ＿ 到 D。

(5) 他把一號和二號一起 ＿ 到 C，再把一號留下，把二號 ＿＿ 到 A。

(6) 他把 1 號從 C ＿ 出來，再 ＿ 到 B。

(7) 他把火車頭開回 C。

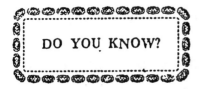
The Rong Bao Zhai Studio

Liulichang is a street in Beijing intimately connected with China's traditional culture and art. The Rongbaozhai Studio is on West Liulichang Street. The studio collects and sells works of famous painters ancient and modern, and is world-renowned for its reproductions of traditional Chinese paintings. The studio has a history of more than 200 years.

Since the founding of the People's Republic of China, the studio has made outstanding achievements in the technique of watercolour block printing, by means of which it has made more than 1,500 reproductions of ancient and modern paintings of various schools ranging from the Tang Dynasty to the present day. Once a painting of shrimps in ink and wash and a reproduction of the work were placed side by side before the famous painter Qi Baishi, "just to give him a quiz". Qi, who himself had done the painting wasn't immediately able to tell which was the original. This is convincing proof of the studio's superb skill in the art of reproduction.

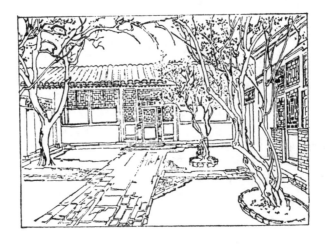

第四十八課

一、課　文

燈　籠　作　好　了

親愛的爸爸、媽媽：

　　因為最近比較忙，所以這封信寫晚了。媽媽著急了吧？

　　我們已經在這兒過了第一個春節。中國的春節就像我們的聖誕節一樣，是全家人團聚的節日。李老師早就請我們到他家去過春節。

　　初一上午，我們到了李老師家。見到他，我們說：“李老師，給您全家拜年！”李老師回答：“祝你們春節好！快到屋裡坐。”他家裡打掃得很乾淨，東西收拾得非常整齊。紅紙黑字的新春聯貼在門上，屋裡牆上還掛著一幅年畫兒。

　　坐下來以後，李老師介紹說：“這是我母親，那是我兒子，叫陽陽。這是黃老師……”陽陽立刻說：“黃老師是我媽媽”。大家都笑了。

　　我把帶來的禮物給了陽陽，他高興地說：“我的燈籠也作

　　　　　　　　(441,442)

好了，我去把它拿來。"黃老師笑著告訴我們："這孩子聽說你們來跟我們一起過年，高興極了，他總問我，應該給外國阿姨什麼新年禮物。我跟他說，你作個燈籠吧⋯⋯"說著，燈籠拿來了，是一隻兔子，上邊還寫著"恭賀新禧"四個字。陽陽問我："阿姨，你喜歡嗎？"我說"作得真好，誰見了都會喜歡的。謝謝你，陽陽。"

這時候，鄰居的孩子正在院子裡放爆竹。他們都穿著新衣服、新鞋，戴著新帽子。一個孩子走過來問古波："叔叔要放爆竹嗎？"古波看著我，我知道他的意思，就說："你什麼都想試一試！別不好意思了，咱們去看看吧。"我們跟陽陽一起走了出來。

古波放了一個爆竹，孩子們高興地鼓掌，讓他再放一個。一會兒黃老師出來說："桌子擺好了，請進來吃飯吧。"

回到屋裡，我們看著桌上這麼多菜，就對黃老師說："太麻煩您了。"她笑了笑，指著正從廚房裡走出來的李老師說："今天的菜是他作的。"真沒想到我們李老師菜作得這麼好。

第一個春節過得很愉快。丁大娘已經跟我們說了，下一個春節一定要在她家過。不多寫了。祝
好

女兒

帕蘭卡二月十九日

(442,443,444)

二、生　詞

1.燈籠	dēnglóng	lantern
燈	dēng	lantern; lamp; light
2.親愛	qīn'ài	dear
3.因為	yīnwei	because; for
4.全	quán	whole
5.團聚	tuánjù	to reunite; to have a reunion
6.節日	jiérì	festival; holiday
節	jié	festival
7.初	chū	a prefix
8.拜年	bài nián	pay a New Year call; wish somebody a happy New Year
年	nián	year; New Year
9.屋（子）	wū (zi)	room
10.打掃	dǎsǎo	to clean up
掃	sǎo	to sweep
11.乾淨	gānjing	clean; neat and tidy
12.收拾	shōushi	to put in order; to tidy up
13.整齊	zhěngqí	neat; tidy
14.黑	hēi	black; dark

15.春聯	chūnlián	Spring Festival couplets; New Year
16.貼	tiē	to paste
17.年畫兒	niánhuàr	New Year (or Spring Festival) picture
18.兒子	érzi	son
19.禮物	lǐwù	gift; present
20.新年	xīnnián	New Year
21.兔子	tùzi	hare; rabbit
22.恭賀新禧	gōnghèxīnxǐ	Happy New Year
23.放(爆竹)	fàng (bàozhu)	to let off (firecrackers)
24.爆竹	bàozhu	firecracker
25.擺	bǎi	to put; to lay (the table)
26.麻煩	máfan	to bother; to put somebody to trouble; troublesome

專　名

1.春節	Chūn Jié	Spring Festival
2.聖誕節	Shèngdàn Jié	Christmas Day
3.黃	Huáng	a surname
4.陽陽	Yángyang	name of a child

補　充　詞

(445,446)

1.除夕	chúxī	New Year's Eve
2.年夜飯	niányèfàn	New Year's Eve family dinner
3.風俗	fēngsú	custom
4.燈節	Dēng Jié	the Lantern Festival (15th of the first month of the lunar calendar)
5.夏曆	xiàlì	the traditional Chinese calendar
6.元宵節	Yuánxiāo Jié	the Lantern Festival
7.袋	dài	bag; sack
8.糧食	liángshi	grain; food

三、閱讀短文

一 家 人

今年春節，解放軍 (jiěfàngjūn the Chinese People's Liberation Army) 戰士 (zhànshì soldier) 王新回北京看母親。

剛下火車，就下雪了。快到家的時候，雪下得更大了。這時候，他看見前邊有一位女同志，她一隻手拿著一袋糧食*，一隻手拿著魚和肉 (ròu meat)，走得很慢。他立刻跑到前邊，說："同志，我幫你拿吧。"

"不用了，很快就到了。"女同志說。

"沒關係，你把糧食給我吧。"王新說著，就把那袋糧食*接過來。

這位女同志看了看王新，就問他：「同志，你去啊兒？」

「回家過春節，我家就在前邊 28 號。」

「你母親是王大娘吧？」

「你怎麼知道……」

「已經到 28 號了，快進去吧！」女同志笑了笑說。

「不，我先把你的東西送去，再回家。」

「你快把糧食拿進去吧，這是……」

王新的母親聽見外邊有人說話，就走了出來。他一看見兒子，就說：「你回來了！啊，蘭英同志也來了。東西快放下，把身上的雪掃掃，到屋裡坐吧。」

走進屋子，王大娘告訴兒子：「這是商店的李蘭英同志，她是來給咱們家送糧食的。她看我歲數大了，你又不在家，每個月都給我把糧食和別的東西買來。」

聽了媽媽的話，王新非常感謝這位售貨員同志。他說：「謝謝你的幫助。」李蘭英說：「不用客氣，你在路上不是也幫助我了嗎？解放軍和人民是一家人啊！」

四、注釋 Notes

1. "我們已經在這兒過了第一個春節。"

The Spring Festival, one of China's traditional holidays, falls on the first day of the first month of the lunar calendar. Hence it is customarily called "New Year".

2. "初一上午，我們到了李老師家。"

The first day of each month in the lunar calendar is referred to as "初一" and the second day as "初二". In fact, all the first ten days of the month are prefixed with "初"; the rest of the days are referred to simply as "十一", "十二", "十三", etc.

3. "給您全家拜年。"

"給……拜年" is a form of greeting used during the New Year or Spring Festival holidays.

4. "上邊還寫著'恭賀新禧'四個字。"

"恭賀新禧" is also a New Year greeting, usually inscribed on New Year cards.

5. "誰見了都會喜歡的。"

The modal particle "的" may be used to denote "certainty" or "doubtlessness", e.g. "明天我一定來的".

6. "太麻煩您了。"

This is an expression used to offer apologies or to thank somebody for the trouble he/she has taken.

五、替換與擴展 Substitution and Extension

㈠

1. 屋子打掃乾淨了嗎？

還沒有打掃乾淨呢。

桌子，擺好	
房間，收拾乾淨	
書， 放整齊	
年畫，掛好	
禮物，買來	
郵票，貼上	

2. <u>春節</u>過得怎麼樣？
  <u>春節</u>過得很<u>愉快</u>。

春聯，寫，漂亮	
燈籠，作，好看	
文章，寫，不錯	
衣服，洗，乾淨	
飯菜，作，好吃	
房間，收拾，整齊	

3. <u>春聯</u>貼在哪兒？
  <u>春聯</u>貼在<u>門</u>上。

花兒，放，客廳裡	
葡萄，種，院子裡	
感想，寫，留言簿上	
菜， 擺，桌子上	

4. 這篇文章有意思嗎?
　　這篇文章很有意思，
　　誰都喜歡看。

這本小説，看
動物園，參觀
北海，　去
太極拳，打
這種語言，學

5. 他什麼都想試一試嗎?
　　他什麼都想試一試。

哪兒，　　　　看
誰，　　　　　問
什麼練習，　　作
哪個公園，　　去
哪位作家的情況，了解

6. 他為什麼沒有回信?
　　因為最近比較忙，所以沒有回信。

上課，　　　病了
回家，　　　學校有事兒
來，　　　　今天過生日
看京劇，　　聽不懂
買那套瓷器，帶的錢不夠

(449,450)

1. Talking about traditional New Year's Eve celebrations:

   Ａ：除夕＊的晚上，你們是怎麼過的？

   Ｂ：我們全家人在一起吃年夜飯＊，那天作了很多菜，喝了酒，還包了餃子。

   Ａ：聽說吃年夜飯＊的時候，桌上都要擺上魚，是嗎？

   Ｂ：對，這也是我們的一種風俗＊。"魚"的發音 (fāyīn pronunciation) 跟 "餘" (yú surplus) 一樣，"年年有魚"，意思就是 "年年有餘" ——大家都希望在新的一年裏生活得更好。

   Ａ：你們睡得很晚嗎？

   Ｂ：睡得很晚。孩子們放爆竹，玩燈籠，都高興得不想睡覺。

2. Talking about letting off firecrackers

   Ａ：春節為什麼要放爆竹？

   Ｂ：放爆竹的意思是送走舊年，迎來新的一年。你知道 "爆竹" 這兩個字是怎麼來的嗎？

   Ａ：不知道。

   Ｂ：很早以前，還沒有現在放的這種爆竹。那時候過春節就燒 (shāo to burn) 竹子，叫 "爆竹"，後來，雖然不再燒竹子了，但是還用這個名字。

3. Talking about the Lantern Festival:

   Ａ：你知道中國的燈節嗎？

   Ｂ：是夏曆＊一月十五吧？

A：對。燈節*又叫元宵節*，那天要吃一種叫作元宵的點心。

B：我在小吃店吃過元宵，非常好吃。

A：除了吃元宵以外，那天還要看燈。一千多年以前就有看燈的風俗*了。

B：好像有一個京劇介紹了古時候燈節*的情況。現在燈節*還能看到燈嗎?

A：能。燈節*那幾天，你在公園裏還可以看到各種燈。

春聯

六、語法　Grammar

1. Notional passive sentences

There are sentences whose subjects are recipients of actions but which have the same structure as sentences whose subjects are performers of actions. Sentences of this type are distinctly passive in meaning, and are called "notional passive sentences". This kind of sentences usually have a subject that refers to a definite person or thing and are frequently used in daily life, e.g.

電影票已經賣完了。

燈籠掛起來了嗎?

菜已經作好了，還沒有拿進去呢。

　　　(452,453,455,456)

2.　The interrogative pronouns of general denotation

Sometimes interrogative pronouns are used not to form questions, but to refer to anybody, anything, or whatever way, and are normally followed by "都" or "也", e.g.

已經十二點了，但是誰也不想睡覺。

他什麼錄音機都能修好。

她家裡哪兒都收拾得很整齊。

箱子裏衣服太多了，箱子蓋兒怎麼也關不上。

3.　The construction "因為…所以…"

In a "因為…所以…" sentence, the "因為" clause names the reason, and the "所以" clause indicates the result.　Sometimes one of the two conjunctions may be omitted, e.g.

因為要準備考試，所以他決定不去旅行了。

他們學習都很努力，所以能學得很好。

因為星期日城裏太擠，他想星期六進城。

七、練習　Exercises

1.　Read aloud the following phrases:

過春節	過聖誕節	過節	過新年
過年	過生日		
比較好	比較近	比較全	
比較舊	比較累	比較小	
比較整齊	比較乾淨	比較正確	

比較豐富　比較清楚

全家　　全班　　全校　　全市　　全國　　全廠

全天　　全年

貼在門上　　掛在牆上　　放在床上

擺在桌上　　拿在手上

2. Turn the following into sentences with a passive meaning:

Example: 她把桌上的東西擺得很整齊。

→桌上的東西擺得很整齊。

(1) 李大娘把院子打掃得很乾淨。

(2) 陽陽把寫著"恭賀新禧"四個大字的燈籠掛在門口。

(3) 王大夫的妻子把飯菜都準備好了。

(4) 他把這件禮物送給了外國阿姨。

(5) 孩子們把爆竹放完了。

(6) 大家很快把餃子包好了。

(7) 王老師把自己寫的春聯貼在門上了。

(8) 他把糖、點心、茶具都擺好了。

3. Use the following phrases to make sentences with a passive meaning:

Example: 準備　飯菜

→過年的飯菜都準備好了。

(1) 買　　禮物

(2) 修　　錄音機

(3) 收拾　　房間

(4) 建設　　工廠

(5) 打掃　　廚房

(6) 寫　文章

(7) 洗　照片

(8) 拿下　鏡頭蓋兒

4. Complete the following sentences with the interrogative pronouns of general denotation given in the brackets:

(1) 兔子這種動物非常可愛，＿＿＿＿。（誰）

(2) 他今天很不舒服，＿＿＿＿。（哪兒）

(3) 因為方向不對，＿＿＿＿。（怎麼）

(4) 這個電影沒有意思，＿＿＿＿。（誰）

(5) 這種糖現在生產得很少，＿＿＿＿。（哪兒）

(6) 天黑了，外邊又沒有燈，＿＿＿＿。（什麼）

(7) 臥室裏除了一張床、一張桌子和兩把椅子以外，＿＿＿＿。（什麼）

(8) 帕蘭卡把古波的自行車騎走了，又沒有告訴他，古波＿＿＿＿。（怎麼）

5. Make up ten questions with "為什麼" on the text, then answer them.

6. Translate the following into Chinese:

(1) The dishes are beautifully laid on the table.（擺）

(2) That was the first time they kept Christmas Day abroad.（過）

(3) He felt rather tired, for he had just played in a ball game.（因為…所以）

(4) Everybody in our class did well in this examination.（全班）

(5) She seldom gets sick. She is rather strong.（比較）

(6) He felt very homesick during the Spring Festival, for it was a holiday for family reunion.（因為…所以…）

(7) He wants to learn everything, but he isn't doing very well in any of his studies.（什麼）

(8)   You can answer this question in whatever way you like. （ 怎麼 ）

7.   Retell the story of the Reading Text with the help of the pictures:

*   *   *

第四十九課

一、課　文

我們都被這個話劇感動了
——古波的日記

四月七日　星期六　（晴）

今天晚上我們全班同學看了話劇《茶館》。我的自行車讓小張借走了，我是坐公共汽車去首都劇場的。

《茶館》是解放以後老舍先生寫的最有名的作品之一。今天的演出非常成功，我們都被它感動了。話劇已經演完了，觀眾還在不停地鼓掌。大家都很激動，誰也不願意離開那兒。觀眾是多麼喜歡老舍的作品，老舍先生被大家叫作"人民藝術家"是多麼正確啊！

老舍不但在中國很有名，而且在我們國家也有很多人知道他。他的小說《駱駝祥子》已經被翻譯成英文、法文，我來中國以前就看過。但是看他的話劇，這還是第一次。

《茶館》寫的是中國舊社會的情況，從一八九八年開始，一共寫了五十年的歷史。老舍先生自己說過："一個大茶館就是一個小社會。"在這個話劇裡我們可以看到：愛國的被抓、被殺，勞動人民沒有吃的，沒有穿的，被逼得賣兒賣女，連茶館的王掌櫃也叫壞人逼得吊死在家裡。這是多麼黑暗的社會啊！

《茶館》不但豐富了我們的歷史知識，而且也加深了我對新中國的了解。以前李老師說過："不了解中國的昨天，就不能很好地了解中國的今天。"他的話是很正確的。

看了今天的話劇，我們都被老舍作品裡的語言吸引住了。我希望以後能有機會研究老舍的語言藝術。

二、生　詞

1. 被　　　　bèi　　　　a preposition

2. 話劇　　　huàjù　　　spoken drama

3. 感動　　　gǎndòng　　to move; to touch; moving

4. 日記　　　rìjì　　　　diary

5. 茶館　　　cháguǎn　　teahouse

6. 讓　　　　ràng　　　　a preposition

7. 借　　　　jiè　　　　to borrow; to lend

8. 劇場　　　jùchǎng　　theatre

9. 作品　　　zuòpǐn　　　works (of literature and art)

10.……之一	…zhīyī	one of…
11.演出	yǎnchū	performance; show; to perform; to put on a show
演	yǎn	to perform; to play; to act
12.成功	chénggōng	to succeed
13.藝術家	yìshùjiā	artist
14.正確	zhèngquè	correct; right
15.不但…而且…	búdàn… érqiě…	not only… but also…
16.社會	shèhuì	society
17.抓	zhuā	to arrest; to catch
18.殺	shā	to kill
19.勞動	láodòng	to labour; to work
20.逼	bī	to force; to compel
21.賣	mài	to sell
22.連…也…	lián…yě…	even…
23.掌櫃	zhǎngguì	shopkeeper
24.叫	jiào	a preposition
25.壞	huài	bad
26.黑暗	hēi'àn	dark
27.吸引	xīyǐn	to attract; to draw

專　名

1. 首都劇場　Shǒudū Jùchǎng　the Capital Theatre
2. 老舍　Lǎo Shě　name of a person
3. 《駱駝祥子》　《Luòtuóxiángzi》 name of a novel

補　充　詞

1. 開演　kāiyǎn　(of a play, movie, etc.) to begin
2. 節目　jiémù　programme; item
3. 説明書　shuōmíngshū　synopsis (of a play or film)
4. 合唱　héchàng　chorus; to chorus
5. 獨唱　dúchàng　solo; to solo
6. 民樂　mínyuè　music, esp. folk music, for traditional instruments
7. 舞蹈　wǔdǎo　dance
8. 女高音　nǚgāoyīn　soprano
9. 演員　yǎnyuán　actor or actress; performer

三、閲讀短文

老舍在倫敦
——訪問老舍夫人

一天上午，我們來到老舍故居，訪問老舍先生的夫人胡絜青 (Hú Jiéqīng)。她給我們談了談老舍在倫敦 (Lúndūn London) 的生活情況。

老舍是從一九二四年開始寫小說的，他最早的三部 (bù a measure word) 小說都是在倫敦寫成的。

胡絜青先生告訴我們，老舍的父親 (fùqin father) 死得很早，他母親給人洗衣服掙點兒錢，家裡非常窮 (qióng poor)。他十九歲就開始教書了。

一九二四年，老舍二十五歲。一位英國朋友介紹他去英國工作，他被倫敦大學請去教中文。老舍除了講課以外，就在學校的圖書館看書，他看了很多英文小說。在看這些文學作品的時候，老舍常常想到自己以前在北京看過和聽過的事兒。他把自己了解的人物和故事都寫在本子上，這就是他的第一部小說《老張的哲學》(《Lǎozhāngdezhéxué》"Lao Zhang's Philosophy of Life")。

後來，作家許地山 (Xǔ Dìshān) 先生到了倫敦，老舍把寫在本子上的故事念給他聽。許地山聽了以後，非常激動地說："好！寫得好！"他把這本小說寄到國內 (guónèi at home; domestic)，很快就發表 (fābiǎo to publish) 了。

聽說老舍先生在倫敦教中文的時候，用北京話錄過音。老舍夫人說："我真想聽聽五十多年前老舍的聲音 (shēngyīn voice) 啊！"

(475,476,477)

四、注釋 Notes

1. "《茶館》是解放以後老舍先生寫的最有名的作品之一。"

Lao She was the pen name of Shu Qingchun, alias Sheyu, a well-known modern Chinese writer of Man nationality (1899−1966). His representative work is "Camel Xiangzi". After the founding of new China, he wrote "The Dragon Beard Ditch", "Teahouse" and a number of other plays, which have enjoyed tremendous popularity among the people. He was honoured with the title of "people's artist".

2. "他的小說《駱駝祥子》已經被翻譯成英文、法文。"

"Camel Xiangzi", one of the best-known modern Chinese novels, was first published in 1937. Set in the Chinese society of the 1930's, the story exposes the evils of the dark days through the vivid description of the tragic experience of the rickshawman Xiangzi.

3. "連茶館的王掌櫃也叫壞人逼得吊死在家裏。"

The adverb "也" may be used for emphasis and is often preceded by "連". "連…也…" means "even...", as in "他連飯也沒有吃就去參加運動會了。"

"掌櫃" was formerly used to refer to a shopkeeper.

五、替換與擴展 Substitution and Extension

(一)

1. 我的自行車讓誰騎走了？
   你的自行車讓他騎走了。

錄音機，	借去
汽車，	開走
照相機，	拿去
本子，	拿錯
爆竹，	放完

2. 這個話劇怎麼樣?

好極了。我們都被它感動了。

```
作品（個），感動
文章（篇），感動
年畫（張），吸引住
小說（篇），吸引住
```

3. 他被大家叫作什麼?

他被大家叫作人民藝術家。

```
選作，車間主任
看作，最熱情的人
叫作，老顧問
```

4. 這個作品被翻譯成英文了嗎?

這個作品還沒有被翻譯成英文。

```
電影（個），中文
小說（本），法文
話劇（個），英文
文章（篇），中文
```

5. 他學習好嗎?

他不但學習好，而且工作也很認真。

聰明,	努力
頭疼,	發燒
會唱歌,	會演話劇
設計過禮堂,	設計過劇場

6. 她很快就走了嗎?

她連茶也沒有喝就走了。

飯,	吃
衣服,	換
話,	說
電視,	看

㈡

1. Going to the theatre

　A：你早就來了吧?

　B：不，我也剛到。咱們進去吧?

　A：幾點開演*?

　B：七點半，還有五分鐘。

　A：咱們的座位在哪兒?

　B：8排6號和8號，從右邊走過去吧。

*　　　*　　　*

A：今天有什麼節目＊？

B：這是說明書＊，你看看。

A：不但有合唱＊、獨唱＊，而且還有民樂＊、舞蹈＊。

B：好極了，我最喜歡聽民樂＊。

2. Talking about impressions

A：你覺得今天的演出怎麼樣？

B：我覺得女高音＊獨唱＊最成功，大家都被她唱的那首民歌吸引住了。我也跟大家一起熱烈地鼓掌。

A：女高音＊很好，可是那個舞蹈＊好像差一點兒，不但演員＊跳得不理想，音樂也不太感動人。

3. Borrowing a book

A：同志，我想借一本老舍的《茶館》。

B：對不起，都被借走了。

A：真不巧 (bù qiǎo unfortunately)！連一本也沒有了嗎？

B：沒有了。你留下姓名，有人還書的時候，我們告訴你，好嗎？

A：謝謝你，你們服務真週到。

*　　　*　　　*

單號	太平門	雙號

六、語法　Grammar

1. "被" sentences

Apart from notional passive sentences, there is another type of passive sentences, known as "被" sentences, formed with the preposition "被", "讓" or "叫". "被" is used mostly in written Chinese; in colloquial speech "讓" and "叫" are more usual. The main verb of a "被" sentence generally contains other elements indicating the result, extent or the time of an action, etc.

"被" sentences are often used to emphasize the passive relationship between the subject and the verb, or to indicate the performer of the action.

Noun or pronoun (receptor)	Preposition "被" "讓" or "叫"	Noun or pronoun (performer)	Verb	Other elements
我的書	讓	他	借	去了。
他的紙	叫	風	颳	走了。
這輛車	被	那位司機	修	好了。
他	被	大家	選	作代表了。
王老師	被	人	請	去講中國文學了。

When it is not necessary to indicate the performer, "被" (but never "讓" or "叫") may be placed immediately before the verb, e.g.

這本書昨天被借走了。

他被選作車間主任了。

If there is a negative adverb or an optative verb in the sentence, it is normally placed before "被", "讓" or "叫", e.g.

(477,478,479)

這本書還沒有被借走。

要是你看了這本小說，也一定會被它吸引住。

2. The construction "不但…而且…"

"不但…而且…" generally occurs in progressive complex sentences. If the two clauses share the same subject (usually appearing in the first clause), "不但" usually goes after the subject. If each clause has its own subject, "不但" and "而且" are normally placed before the two subjects respectively, e.g.

他不但是我的好老師，而且也是我的好朋友。

這個話劇不但寫得好，而且演得也很成功。

不但中國人懷念這位藝術家，而且外國人也懷念他。

不但古波和帕蘭卡沒有去過茶館，而且連小張也沒有去過。

七、練習 Exercises

1. Read aloud the following phrases:

被這個故事感動了　　感動了大家　　很感動　　感動人

被它吸引住了　　吸引了大家　　很吸引人

演出話劇　　演出京劇　　看演出　　成功的演出

演話劇　　演得很成功　　演了兩個多小時　　演王掌櫃

勞動人民　　喜歡勞動　　參加勞動　　勞動了一年

壞人　　壞事　　壞天氣　　壞衣服　　寫壞　　用壞

2. Change the following sentences from the passive voice into the active voice:

(1) 大家都被這個電影感動了。

(2) 這本小説被她翻譯成法文了。

(3) 小説《李自成》讓小張借走了。

(4) 帕蘭卡被古波送到北京醫院去了。

(5) 老舍先生被大家叫作"人民藝術家"。

(6) 買來的冰棍兒都讓孩子們吃完了。

3. Change the following "把" sentences into "被" sentences, making other necessary changes:

(1) 工人們把那些活兒幹完了。

(2) 同學們把我們的行李拿到宿舍去了。

(3) 古波把小張保持的記錄打破了。

(4) 那位老工人把我的自行車修好了。

(5) 李老師把這位新同學介紹給大家。

(6) 進步青年把魯迅先生看作自己的老師。

4. Complete the following sentences:

(1) 這兒的春天不但很冷，而且還 _____ 。

(2) 老舍先生不但寫了很多小説，而且還 _____ 。

(3) 學過的漢字不但應該會唸，而且 _____ 。

(4) 老師不但 _____ ，而且非常關心我們的身體。

(5) 不但中國人喜歡看《大鬧天宮》這個電影，而且 _____ 。

(6) 他不但夏天常常去頤和園，而且 _____ 。

(7) 他的漢語水平很高，連 _____ 也能看懂。

(8) 代表團在北京的時間很短，連 _____ 也沒有去。

5. Translate the following into Chinese:

   (1) This is one of the best-known new Chinese films. （之一）

   (2) These tasks have been accomplished by the three of them. （被）

   (3) He seldom goes to see a play. He does not even know where the Capital Theatre is. （連…也…）

   (4) The bottle of wine was drunk all up by them. （讓）

   (5) Not only has he met the artist himself, he has also chatted with him.

   (6) He not only writes his letters in Chinese, but also keeps a diary in Chinese. （不但…而且…）

   (7) The works of that young writer are very moving. （感動）

   (8) The chair was taken out to the courtyard by me. （被）

6. Read the following story, then retell it.

      一天，阿凡提 (Āfántí *name of a person*) 被他朋友請到家裏吃晚飯。客人們都來了，他朋友為客人準備了很多好吃的東西。

      坐在阿凡提旁邊的一位客人，吃東西吃得又多又快。在別人不注意的時候，他把一些好吃的東西放進自己的口袋 (kǒudài *pocket*) 裏。這事兒被阿凡提看見了。

      阿凡提拿起茶壺，把茶水倒 (dào *to pour*) 進那個人的口袋裏。

      "阿凡提，您怎麼了？您想幹什麼？"

      "您的口袋吃了那麼多的東西，一定很想喝水。我想讓它喝點兒茶。"

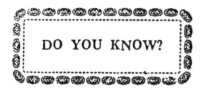

DO YOU KNOW?

Main Dynasties in China's History

夏 Xià	c.21st–16th century B.C.	唐 Táng	618 – 907
商 Shāng	c.16th–11th century B.C.	五代 Wǔdài	907 – 960
周 Zhōu	c.11th century-256 B.C.	宋 Sòng	960 – 1279
秦 Qín	221–206 B.C.	遼 Liáo	907 – 1125
漢 Hàn	206 B.C.–220	金 Jīn	1115 – 1234
三國 Sānguó	220–280	元 Yuán	1271 – 1368
晉 Jìn	265–420	明 Míng	1368 – 1644
南北朝 Nán-Běi Cháo	420–589	清 Qīng	1644 – 1911
隋 Suí	581–618		

(486)

第五十課

復 習

一、課 文

心 中 的 花 兒

　　昨天在中國美術館，我參觀了一個畫展。有一幅畫兒，畫的是蘭花，前邊站了很多人，我也走了過去。臨摹這幅畫兒的人真不少，最讓人注意的是一個十二、三歲的小姑娘。她畫得非常認真，一會兒看看那幅畫兒，一會兒在自己的本子上一筆一筆地畫。蘭花很快就畫好了，我和旁邊的人看了都說："小姑娘畫得真不錯！"

　　休息的時候我又見到那個小姑娘。我走過去問她："能把你的畫兒給我看看嗎？"她不好意思地笑了，小聲地對我說："畫得不好，請您提提意見吧。"說著，把本子給了我。我打開第一頁，上邊貼著一張周恩來總理的照片。那是周總理逝世前幾天照的，我在很多中國人的家裡都看到過這張照片。第二頁畫了一枝挺立的紅蓮，旁邊還寫著"周總理逝世一週年"。

我又看第三頁，也是花兒，畫的是風雪中的紅梅。我立刻想到了陳毅的《紅梅》詩。第四頁是迎春花，第五頁、第六頁……都是花兒。最後是她剛畫的蘭花。"這麼多花兒，你要畫個大花園嗎？"我問她。小姑娘笑著說："我還沒畫完呢。我不但要畫中國的花兒，還要畫外國的花兒。我要把世界上最美的花兒畫在一起，讓周總理永遠站在花海中微笑。"

二、生　詞

1.	畫展	huàzhǎn	art exhibition
2.	蘭花	lánhuā	cymbidium; orchid
3.	臨摹	línmó	to copy (a model of callingraphy or painting)
4.	筆	bǐ	a measure word
5.	打開	dǎ kāi	to open
6.	頁	yè	page; a measure word, page
7.	總理	zǒnglǐ	premier
8.	逝世	shìshì	to pass away
9.	枝	zhī	a measure word
10.	挺立	tǐnglì	to stand erect; to stand up-right
11.	紅蓮	hónglián	red lotus
12.	週年	zhōunián	anniversary

13.迎春花	yíngchūnhuā	winter jasmine
14.最後	zuìhòu	last
15.世界	shìjiè	the world
16.海	hǎi	sea
17.微笑	wēixiào	to smile

專　名

1.中國美術館	Zhōngguó Měishùguǎn	National Art Gallery
2.周恩來	Zhōu Ēnlái	name of a person
3.周總理	Zhōu Zǒnglǐ	Premier Zhou

心 中 的 花 兒

三、注釋 Notes

1. "最讓人注意的是一個十二、三歲的小姑娘。"

"十二、三歲" means "between 12 and 13 years old". Two successive numerals are often used to give an approximate number, as in "七、八本書", "去過兩、三次", "五、六千個學生", etc.

2. "一會兒在自己的本子上一筆一筆地畫。"

"Now she... now she made one stroke after another in her writing pad."

The repeated form of a numeral-measure word group is often used adverbially to indicate manner, e.g. "他把學過的課文一篇一篇地復習了一遍。" "他們兩個兩個地練習問答。"

四、看圖會話 Talk About These Pictures

1. 請你把……

2. ···被···

五、語法小結　**A Brief Summary of Grammar**

1.　Sentences with a verbal predicate (2)

(1)　Sentences with "是···的"

　　她是跟貿易代表團來的。

　　那幅畫兒不是今年臨摹的。

　　他們倆是在李老師家過的春節。

(2)　Existential sentences

　　後邊開過來一輛汽車。

　　桌子旁邊沒有擺著椅子。

　　劇場前邊站著很多人。

(3) "把" sentences

古波把信給她了。

請大家不要把花兒擠壞。

你把他送到家了嗎?

他把這幅畫兒賣給了一個外國人。

(4) "被" sentences

老舍先生被大家叫作 "人民藝術家"。

這個足球叫他們踢壞了。

那本書讓古波借走了。

誰來了都會被這兒的風景吸引住。

2. Some structures used in complex sentences

(1) Coordination

"有的…有的…"

郵局裏人很多,有的坐著寫信,有的等著寄東西。

這位青年作家的作品,有的我喜歡,有的我不喜歡。

"又…又…"

顧客走進來都希望吃得又好,花錢又少。

魯迅先生又是青年的好老師,又是青年的好朋友。

(2) Condition

"要是…就…"

要是天氣好，就能看得更遠。

你要是不太忙，咱們就到外邊走走吧。

"一…就…"

她一看見帕蘭卡，就說照片上的阿姨來了。

我一著急，就把這件事兒忘了。

"只有…才…"

只有星期天才有空兒出來玩兒。

只有把錄音機打開檢查一下兒，才能知道哪兒壞了。

(3) Cause and result

"因為…所以…"

因為最近比較忙，所以這封信寫晚了。

他病得很厲害，所以立刻被送到了醫院。

(4) Transition

"雖然…但是…"

他雖然老了，但是還願意多作一些工作。

雖然我們認識的時間不長，但是互相很了解。

(5) Progression

"不但…而且…"

這位藝術家不但在中國很有名，而且在世界上也很有名。

不但看這幅畫兒的人很多，而且臨摹的人也不少。

(494,495,496)   — 316 —

(6) Inclusion and exclusion
"除了…以外"

除了一張床以外，還有一張舊桌子和兩把椅子。

老舍寫的話劇，除了《茶館》以外，他都沒看過。

3. The adverbs "又" and "也"
   "又" may be used to indicate:
(1) That an action is repeated

我們又認識了兩位年輕的朋友。

他昨天沒有來，今天又沒有來。

(2) Two things of opposite nature

熊貓頭非常大，耳朵又這麼小。

你很喜歡看畫展，怎麼又不想去了？

(3) The meaning of "in addition to"

古波把信給他，又把桌子上的錄音機開開。

他進城參觀了畫展，又看了一個電影。

(4) The simultaneous existence of two different circumstances

我又餓又累。

今天很熱，又沒有風。

"也" may be used to indicate:
(1) Some kind of similarity or resemblance

－ 317 －

他也學習漢語嗎?

他喜歡蘭花，我也喜歡蘭花。

(2)　Emphasis

連王掌櫃也被逼得吊死了。

看這個電影，古波也感動得哭了。

六、練習　Exercises

1.　Give nouns that may be modified by the following measure words:

個：＿＿＿＿＿＿＿＿　　張：＿＿＿＿＿＿＿＿

件：＿＿＿＿＿＿＿＿　　條：＿＿＿＿＿＿＿＿

套：＿＿＿＿＿＿＿＿　　座：＿＿＿＿＿＿＿＿

句：＿＿＿＿＿＿＿＿　　本：＿＿＿＿＿＿＿＿

雙：＿＿＿＿＿＿＿＿　　隻：＿＿＿＿＿＿＿＿

2.　Make up "把" sentences with the following phrases:

Example:　打掃　　屋子　　乾淨

　　　　　→我們把屋子打掃乾淨了。

(1)　建設　　自己的國家　　好

(2)　檢查　　練習　　一遍

(3)　保持　　記錄　　三年

(4)　穿　　鞋　　壞了

(5)　掛　　年畫　　在牆上

(6)　想　　這個問題　　一下兒

(7) 帶　　　《野草》　　來

(8) 留　　　東西　　　在家裡

(9) 洗　　　衣服　　　乾淨

(10) 擺　　　花兒　　　在桌子上

3. Turn the following "把" sentences into "被" sentences, making other necessary changes:

(1) 老師把我們的問題一個一個地講解清楚了。

(2) 這位大夫把他的病看好了。

(3) 他女兒把郵票收在箱子裏了。

(4) 我把一塊錢換成了兩張五毛的。

(5) 他把這束迎春花畫在紙上了。

(6) 大家把七、八本《茶館》都借走了。

4. Fill in the blanks with appropriate conjunctions:

(1) _____ 我們坐在前邊，_____ 聽得很清楚。

(2) _____ 他歲數大了，_____ 眼睛非常好。

(3) 你 _____ 早來五分鐘，_____ 能看見他。

(4) _____ 中國人過春節，_____ 別的亞洲國家有的也過春節。

(5) _____ 我聽不懂廣州話，_____ 北京人也聽不懂廣州話。

(6) _____ 先學好漢語，_____ 能學好專業。

5. Translate the following into Chinese:

(1) They have come to wish their teacher a happy New Year.
（是…的）

(2) It was during last Spring Festival that we had a family reunion.
（是…的）

(3) Many cars were parked outside the hospital. （停著）

(4) He was standing outdoors with very little clothes on. That's why he

felt cold. (又)

(5) He is a great man, yet he lives a simple life. (又)

(6) We liked this art exhibition very much. Mr. Li, our teacher, was also fascinated by it. (也)

(7) This park is awful. There aren't even many flowers. (連…也)

(8) He translated this text into French sentence by sentence.
(一句一句地)

6. Correct the following sentences:

(1) 他放那封信在桌上。

(2) 孩子們把故事聽高興了。

(3) 我同學把練習作得很認真。

(4) 我把那個人認識了。

(5) 我們應該把他幫助。

(6) 他把本子沒找到。

(7) 我朋友把一本書送給我了。

(8) 練習已經被作完了。

(9) 我把這件事兒作得好。

(10) 我被這個話劇沒有感動。

7. Write a composition about your Chinese studies.

七、語音語調 Pronunciation and Intonation

1. Logical stress

Logical stress is the type of stress put on a certain syllables in order to give prominence to the main idea of a sentence. The same sentence may convey different meanings with logical stress placed on different syllables. E.g.

我知道你喜歡老舍的話劇。（別人不一定知道）

我知道你喜歡老舍的話劇。（你不用告訴我了）

我知道你喜歡老舍的話劇。（別人喜歡不喜歡我不知道）

我知道你喜歡老舍的話劇。（你怎麼說不喜歡呢）

我知道你喜歡老舍的話劇。（還喜歡不喜歡別人的話劇我不知道）

我知道你喜歡老舍的話劇。（喜歡不喜歡老舍的小説我不知道）

2.　Sense group stress

(1)　In "把" sentences, the object following the verb is usually stressed. E.g.

古波把信給了她。

他把這張照片送給了魯迅。

(2)　When the verb is followed by both a complement and an object, the object is stressed. E.g.

古波把她送到了醫院。

她把感想寫在留言簿上。

(3)　A long "把" sentence may be divided into several sense groups. The preposition "把" and its object may form one of the sense group. The object of the preposition "把" is stressed. E.g.

北京人把這種房子 / 叫作"老虎尾巴"。

進步青年把魯迅先生 / 看作自己的好老師。

我把最大的 / 給你帶來了。

3. Read aloud the following allegory:

公鷄和狐狸

一天，狐狸(húli fox) 看到公鷄(gōngjī cock)，它很熱情地説：“我親愛的朋友，你好嗎？”

公鷄説：“謝謝你，我很好。你呢？”

狐狸説：“謝謝你，我也很好。你知道嗎，現在所有(suǒyǒu all) 的動物都是朋友了？”

公鷄説：“那好極了，好極了！”

狐狸説：“你不到我家來嗎？讓我們一起吃早飯吧。”

“好吧。”公鷄説，“你看，那邊來了一隻狗 (gǒu dog)，讓我們也請它來吃早飯吧！”

“狗？”狐狸頭也不回就走了。

公鷄笑着説：“我親愛的狐狸，你到哪兒去呀？你不喜歡狗嗎？不是所有的動物都是朋友了嗎？”